W9-ARS-220

17 Reasons to Lighten Up and Laugh More

a tribute to

Leslie B. Flynn

Leslie B. Flynn, devoted Baptist minister, teacher, and prolific author, went home to heaven in August, 2006 at the age of 87. Born in Ontario, Canada, in 1918, he received a BA from Wheaton College in 1942, and, after earning a BD and an MA, was granted a Doctor of Divinity from Denver Seminary in 1963. A pastor for more than 45 years—the last 40 at Grace Baptist Church in Nanuet, New York—he began writing articles in the late 1940s and soon turned to book writing. Leslie was passionate about ministering the truth of God's Word to Christians everywhere.

Some of his 43 books have been translated by Christian publishers around the world. Leslie will be missed by all who have grown in Christ from reading his writings.

Here's a partial list of books he wrote:
19 Gifts of the Spirit
Did I Say That?
The Twelve
The Gift of Joy
The Sustaining Power of Hope

Published by Magnus Press:
Jesus in the Image of God: A Challenge to Christlikeness
What the Church Owes the Jew
Keep On Keeping On
Thanks! Seeing God's World with a Grateful Heart
Laugh! 17 Reasons to Lighten Up and Laugh More

Thanks, Leslie!

17 Reasons to
Lighten Up and Laugh More

Leslie B. Flynn

MAGNUS PRESS

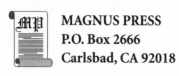

MAGNUS PRESS
P.O. Box 2666
Carlsbad, CA 92018

www.magnuspress.com

Laugh! 17 Reasons to Lighten Up and Laugh More

Copyright © 2007 by The Flynn Family Trust

All Rights Reserved. No part of this book may be reproduced in any form without written permission from the publisher.

First Edition, 2007

Printed in the United States of America

All Scripture quotations, unless otherwise noted, are taken from the Holy Bible, NEW INTERNATIONAL VERSION. Copyright©1973, 1978, 1984 by International Bible Society. Used by permission of the International Bible Society.

LCCN: 2006935280
ISBN: 978-0-9724869-4-1

Publisher's Cataloging-in-Publication
(Prepared by The Donohue Group, Inc.)

Flynn, Leslie B.
    Laugh! : 17 reasons to lighten up and laugh more / by Leslie B.
Flynn. -- 1st ed.

    p. : ill. ; cm.

    Includes bibliographical references.
    ISBN: 978-0-9724869-4-1

1. Laughter--Religious aspects--Christianity. 2. Wit and humor--Religious aspects--Christianity. 3. Joy--Religious aspects--Christianity. 4. Life--Anecdotes. 5. Life--Humor. I. Title.

BV4647.J68 F59 2007
248.4   2006935280

11 10 09 08 07   10 9 8 7 6 5 4 3 2 1

To the

Carlson family of Wheaton, Illinois

Shirley

Kenneth, Gisela, and Bernt

Mark, Nancy, David, and Beth

Keith, Ruth, Bryan, and Brad

Allen, Karen, Kristen, and Erik

Linda and Theodore (Witte)

who often win the prize for the most humorous float

at the Fourth of July parade, a Carlson tradition for

more than 90 years

CONTENTS

PREFACE

When I was a student for the ministry, I recall swapping jokes around the breakfast table. Invariably, at some pause a good brother would look up from his New Testament, clear his throat, and intone in a voice that seemed to come from the bottom of a grave in a fog-shrouded cemetery, "Remember, brethren, 'Every idle word that men shall speak, they shall give account thereof in the day of judgment.'" That put a damper on any more jokes—till the next morning.

Through the centuries humor has often been suspect in Christian circles. Even today many associate a smiling face with a shallow disposition, assuming "all virtue lies in gravity, and smiles are symptoms of depravity."[1]

Often those fixated on gloom and doom remind us that Jesus never laughed, and that the apostle Paul condemned foolish speaking. The truth is that Jesus and Paul did use humor, and its proper use may well reflect the joy and forti-tude of a Spirit-filled life. German theologian Helmut

Thielicke said, "Should we not see that lines of laughter about the eyes are just as much marks of faith as are the lines of care and seriousness?"[2]

This book lists 17 biblical reasons why we should not bury our fondness for humor, but rather appreciate, develop, and exercise our sense of wit. We are fully aware that analyzing humor has been likened to dissecting a frog. (Few people are interested; the frog dies of the process; and besides we're left with a mess.) Since most people prefer hearing jokes rather than explanations or autopsies of why something is funny, we have made our analyses of these 17 reasons brief and concise. And, in addition, we have devoted far more space to a supply of humorous items to enjoy, coming from personal, family, and church life.

Well-known Baptist preacher Charles Haddon Spurgeon and a pastor friend were walking in the English countryside, chatting and chuckling in high spirits. One told a story that made them both laugh uproariously. Spurgeon suddenly turned and said, "Let's kneel down and thank God for laughter." There under the sky two great spirits knelt and thanked God for the joyous gift of laughter.

Hilarity and holiness can indeed dwell together in harmony. We need to lighten up and laugh more.

Chapter 1

HUMOR'S HEAVENLY ORIGIN

A 40-year-old Virginia woman, with three children in school, learned she was again pregnant. Her shock turned to genuine delight. Soon after, to her amazement, her 20-year-old married daughter in Ohio phoned to say that she, too, was pregnant with her first baby. When they came together at a joint shower, mother and daughter giggled like sisters. Later the mother wrote, "Sometime this month, if all goes according to plan, I'll be a mother and a grandmother. Maybe on the same day, if the Lord has a sense of humor. I can already see Him grinning."[3]

Whether or not they became mother and grandmother on the same day, God does have a sense of humor. The Bible ascribes laughter to God. Says the Psalmist, "The One enthroned in heaven laughs" (2:4). The late Fuller Theological Seminary Professor Paul K. Jewett said in a chapel talk, "Milton is bold enough in *Paradise Lost* to put a jest on the lips of deity. When Lucifer and the angels revolted, with grim humor the Almighty declared, 'Nearly it now concerns us to be sure of our omnipotence. . .'"(V, 721-22).[4]

Maybe theologians should have listed humor among the attributes of God. Dean Inge, once leading cleric of the Church of England, said, "I have never understood why it should be considered derogatory to the Creator to suppose that He has a sense of humor."[5]

Wit is related to wisdom. Wisdom involves the recognition of things harmonious; wit involves the awareness of things incongruous. Made in the image of the all-wise God, humans who easily recognize order in life should also be apt at spotting absurdities. He who is wise should be witty. Norman Cousins said, "Of all the gifts bestowed by nature on human beings, hearty laughter must be close to the top. The response to incongruities is one of the highest manifestations of the cerebral process. . . . The brain accommodates itself to the collision of logic and absurdity by finding an outlet in the physiological response we recognize as laughter."[6]

Since God made us in His likeness, He bestowed on us the capacity for humor. This is why of all creatures in the world only humans can laugh. So we should not be surprised when we discover, according to a Bible teacher of a previous century, that God in His written word to mankind, the Bible, makes use of "the whole armory of humor—wit, satire, irony, retort, ridicule, drollery, play on words."[7]

Yes, our sense of humor comes from heaven above. So, let's lighten up and laugh more.

• • •

BABIES

Five-year-old Bobby told his dad he'd like to have a baby brother. His dad, knowing that his wife was expecting in a couple of months, replied, "If you pray for a baby brother every night for the next two months, I guarantee that God will give you one." That night Bobby began praying, but after praying every night for a whole month he became weary and stopped praying.

A month later his mother went to the hospital. When she came home, his father called him into the bedroom to see the little bundle lying next to his mother. Pulling back the covers to reveal, not just one, but *two* baby brothers, his dad said, "Now, aren't you glad you prayed?"

Bobby answered, "Aren't you glad I quit when I did?"

• • •

Noting that the chores of caring for their three-month-old baby seemed to be weighing heavily on his wife, her husband decided to cheer her up. "Remember, darling, the hand that rocks the cradle rules the world."

Handing him a diaper, she said, "Take over the world for two hours while I get my hair done."

• • •

A mother came home from the hospital with her new baby still wearing the hospital identification tag. The mother's five-year old son met his new little brother, then asked, "Mom, when are you gonna take off his price tag?"

• • •

MOTHERS

Larry's Sunday school teacher patted him on the head and asked, "Is your mother still as pretty as she used to be?"

"Oh yeah," said Larry. "It just takes her a lot longer."

• • •

After a Sunday morning service a mother related how she was able to get her fidgety, seven-year-old son to settle down and sit still. "About halfway through the sermon I whisper, 'If you don't be quiet, the pastor will lose his place and will have to start his sermon all over again.'"

• • •

The department store was crowded with shoppers. A young mother had the added difficulty of a small daughter pulling at her side and whimpering incessantly. Suddenly the harassed mother pleaded softly, "Quiet, Susanna, just calm yourself and take it easy."

An admiring clerk commented on the mother's psychology, then turned to the child, "So, your name is Susanna."

"Oh, no," interrupted the mother. "Her name's Joan. I'm Susanna."

• • •

A mother of two was talking about her neighbor who had seven children. "She's fabulous. She's unbelievable. She keeps her house spotless. She sews all the kids' clothes. She's a good cook. Her children are smart, active and polite. She is active in church and the Girl Scouts. She's good-looking and vivacious. She makes me sick!"

• • •

PARENTS

Be thankful for small children who put away their playthings and clean up after themselves. They're such a joy you hate to see them go home to their own parents.

• • •

Eastern proverb: "If thine enemy wrong thee, give each of his children a drum."

• • •

The best years of a parent's life are when the kids are old

enough to help shovel the driveway, but still too young to drive the car.

• • •

A mother asked her two-year old to take his dirty clothes and put them in the hamper. The lad looked puzzled, so she explained, "You know—the place we put our dirty clothes before they're washed."

Her son picked up his clothes, trotted into his parents' bedroom, dragging them beside him, and then dropped them on the floor—right by his father's side of the bed.

• • •

VALENTINE'S DAY

Two seminary students were looking through Valentine cards in a nearby store. One said, "Here's a card that says, 'To the only girl I've ever really loved.'"

His roommate exclaimed, "Oh, I'm going to buy a dozen."

• • •

VISITATION

A new pastor and his bride had just been called to a new and larger church. Wishing to get a good start, they started out visiting the members, family by family. They were directed to the home of one of the church pillars, an elderly widow of means, though not known for her housekeeping abilities.

They took along their only child at the time, their two-year-old, a lively girl who, soon after arrival, ran her fingers across the dusty floor, held them up, and shouted out, "Dirty, dirty, dirty!"

The pastor and his wife thought their ministry was now ruined, but they discovered that this lady was quite deaf. They stayed for four decades.

• • •

A deacon, presenting the church's farewell gift to their pastor, who was going to another church: "He was a diligent visitor among his flock, and many homes were happy when he left."

• • •

A minister on visitation one afternoon knocked at a door several times, but no one answered. Seeing through the curtain that the TV was on, he wrote on the back of his calling card, "Revelation 3:20," and left it in the mail box. (Revelation 3:20 says, "Behold I stand at the door and knock. If anyone hears my voice and opens the door, I will come in. . .")

Next Sunday, as people were leaving the church, a lady handed the pastor a card with her name and "Genesis 3:10" written on it. Back in his study he looked up the reference and read, "I heard thy voice and I was afraid because I was naked, so I hid myself."

• • •

The pastor had just comfortably settled in an easy chair when little Susie came running into the living room.

Wishing to make a good impression on her visiting pastor, the mother told the child, "Please go get that book your mother just loves to read."

A minute later Susie came back lugging the big Sears catalog.

• • •

A pastor received a phone call from a lady he had never met, and who was not a member of his church but very active in a church of another denomination across town. She said she was ill and would appreciate a visit at her home.

When he arrived, the pastor said to the lady's ten-year-old

son, "I'm happy your mother called me. Only tell me—is your minister out of town?"

"No," replied the little lad. "Mommy just said she was afraid she might have a sickness that was contagious."

• • •

Chapter 2

GOD'S WHIMSICAL WAYS

A pastor wasn't too happy with his youth minister for inviting an aspiring rock group to play at a youth rally. Not accustomed to the loud noise of the band, he gritted his teeth through the evening, planning to express his disapproval at the next staff meeting. At the invitation, to his amazement, his wayward daughter came forward and accepted Christ. The youth minister smiled to himself, "God certainly has a sense of humor." The pastor's daughter lived a changed life thereafter.

The Lord often works wonders in an unlikely, amusing, whimsical way. He often makes mischief boomerang on the mischief-maker. A man falls into the pit he dug for another. Haman, who built gallows on which to hang Mordecai, an innocent Jew, was hanged on his own gallows (Est. 7:10). Those who plotted to throw Daniel into the lions' den were themselves tossed in (Dan. 6:24).

The Lord employs the foolish, lowly, and weak to confound the wise, the high, and the mighty. He used a slender rod in Moses' hand to part the Red Sea (Ex. 14:16). He used a donkey to get a message to Balaam (Num. 22:28). He used a small stone, slung by the boy David, to strike the giant Goliath a mortal blow (1 Sam. 17:48-50).

No human could ever have dreamed up the story of God's forgiveness through the death of His Son by crucifixion, an ignominious death reserved for criminals, foreigners and slaves. Paul wrote, "The message of the cross is foolishness to those who are perishing" (1 Cor. 1:18). But to those who believe, this foolish message has become "the power of God" (v.19). The cross is no longer an emblem of shame, but of glory.

Heavenly practices often reverse earthly methodology and values. In God's upside-down kingdom, whoever exalts self will be abased, but whoever humbles self will be exalted. In the celestial banking system, the more we keep, the less we have. And the more we give, the more we keep. A worldly person is sometimes miserable in the midst of his seeming joys, the Christian joyful in the midst of his miseries. God's strength is made perfect in weakness. Those who indulge in license end up slaves, but those who walk the narrow way as slaves of Christ find liberty.

Grace, God's unmerited favor, is incredible. It comes to us a free gift from God, dropped into our hands! Where sin abounds, grace does much more abound. The prodigal son is surrounded by the father's love. Chief-of-sinners Saul is struck down by the risen Christ, forgiven, and commissioned chief apostle to the Gentiles. Perhaps the popular song "Amazing Grace" could also be titled, "Laughable Grace."

Let's laugh at God's whimsical ways.

• • •

ADVERSITY

Max was driving in downtown New York. Late for a crucial business meeting, he had a problem. He was looking for a parking spot but couldn't find one. No matter where he tried, every place was taken. He was frantic. In desperation he looked heavenward and prayed, "God, if you give me a parking spot, I promise I'll never again skip church to attend a football game. I'll double my pledge for missions, and I'll join a Habitat for Humanity team next summer." Suddenly, a parking space opened up right in front of him. Max gazed up to heaven and said, "Never mind, I just found one."

• • •

Christians should be like tea kettles, which, when the pressure is on, don't whine but whistle.

• • •

Don't let worries get you down. Remember—Moses was a basket case!

• • •

When Winston Churchill lost the election in Britain back in 1946, his wife said to him that it was a blessing in disguise.

He replied, "If it's a blessing, it's well-disguised."

• • •

A wife took a trip through Europe, leaving her invalid mother at home with her husband. Stopping at London, Paris, Rome, and Athens, at each place she telephoned home. At the last stop, Athens, her husband informed her that her dog had died. She reacted by saying that he should not have broken the news so suddenly but should have broken it to her gradually.

Then she went on to inform him how he should have done it. When she called from London, he should have said that the dog was on the roof. When in Paris, that the dog had fallen off the roof. When in Rome, that the dog was very bad. And finally in Athens, inform her of the dog's death.

Then the wife asked her husband how her mother was. Replied the husband, "She's on the roof."

• • •

FAMOUS PEOPLE

Fame is a funny business. One week you're on the cover of *Time*. And the next week you're doing it.

• • •

Winston Churchill, featured speaker at an important banquet, was not introduced till after a long, tedious program, and very late in the evening. Rising, he said, "I have been asked to give a short address, and here it is, '10 Downing Street,' and I'm going there right now."

• • •

Dr. Ralph Abernathy, a civil rights leader associated with Dr. Martin Luther King, Jr., was a scheduled speaker at the 1967 U.S. Congress on Evangelism held in Minneapolis. Security precautions, because of threats on his life, caused a substantial delay in his arrival to address the several thousand present. His opening remark soothed the unrest. He began, "I'd rather be Ralph Abernathy late than the late Ralph Abernathy."

• • •

The well-known German author, Goethe, and equally famous composer, Beethoven, were out walking one afternoon. Everywhere they went, people pointed them out. Goethe exclaimed, "Isn't this maddening? I simply can't escape this homage!"

Beethoven replied, "Don't be too distressed by it. It's just possible that some of it may be for me."

• • •

It was a dramatic moment in the final rehearsal for the coronation of Queen Elizabeth II. The orchestra's final strains had sounded, the archbishop stood by the altar, and nearby were the officials of state. Then sounded the spine-tingling fanfare of trumpets. The queen was about to enter.

Suddenly, instead, into this awesome scene pranced four charwomen, palace maids in white overalls, waving four carpet sweepers. The vast assembly, present for the rehearsal, burst into laughter long and hard, and with no disrespect for the splendid pageantry of royalty.

• • •

An airline attendant, checking to make sure the passengers all had their seat belts fastened for take-off, came across Mohammed Ali, former world's heavyweight boxing champion. She reminded him to buckle up.

Ali replied, "Superman don't need no seat belt."

She responded, "Superman don't need no airplane, either. Buckle up."

• • •

Saddam Hussein had a statue of himself built alongside one of Nebuchadnezzar in Babylon, hinting that his military prowess was on a par with the great ancient king and conqueror of ancient history.

When a reporter asked General Schwarzkopf at the end of the Gulf War what he thought of Saddam's leadership, he noted, ticking off his contempt on the fingers of his left hand, that Saddam was "neither a strategist, nor is he schooled in the operational art, nor is he a tactician, nor is he a general, nor is he a soldier."

Having run out of fingers, he said, "Other than that, he is a great military man."

• • •

GOVERNMENT

From a letter to a deceased person from the Greenville, South Carolina, Department of Social Services: "Your food stamps will be stopped, effective immediately, because we received notice that you passed away. May God bless you. You may reapply if there is a change in your circumstances."

• • •

A one-time Chaplain of the Senate, Rev. Edward Hale, was asked if he prayed for the Senators.

"No," he replied, "I look at the Senators and pray for the nation."

• • •

MIRACLES

A schoolteacher tried to convince one of her sixth-graders that what she had learned in Sunday school about Moses leading the Israelites through the Red Sea was no miracle. "It was nothing out of the ordinary," explained the skeptical teacher. "Actually Moses and the Israelites simply walked across a two-inch deep marsh called the Red Sea."

The bright sixth-grader responded, "Wow! Then the Lord really did save the day when he drowned the whole Egyptian army in a little puddle of water."

• • •

PRAYER

Prayer meeting was almost over. The pastor thought he would ask a member of the board to close in prayer. "Deacon

Jones, will you please lead?"

Silence. Deacon Jones had fallen asleep. His wife nudged him just as the pastor repeated his request, "Deacon Jones, will you please lead?"

"Lead?" stammered the confused deacon, coming to consciousness. "I just dealt."

• • •

During the sermon a father became annoyed with the misbehavior of his five-year old son, who was getting disapproving stares from nearby worshipers. Suddenly the exasperated father picked up his son and started down the aisle.

Looking back over his father's shoulder, the little fellow interrupted the sermon by calling out a desperate plea to the congregation, "Please pray for me!"

• • •

Chapter 3

GOD'S COMICAL CREATURES

God has populated our world with creatures that He knew
would tickle our sense of humor. Earth, sea, and sky are filled
with creatures that seem more designed for play than work, like
the frolicking leviathan (Ps. 104:26). Tourists to Hawaii like to
watch the whales breaching close to shore in Pacific waters.

The various faces in God's animal kingdom entertain us,
some scary, or wary, or hairy with tufts, or mustaches, or
beards or whiskers. Beaks come in all shapes, as do fancy
plumes with ornamental feathers. A little boy back from the
zoo described one bird as resembling "the hat worn by the lady
that sits in front of us in church."

Surely God himself must have smiled as He designed some
of these creatures long ago. At the beginning, He announced
His divine approval over all forms of nature, including the
amusing and playful, calling them all "good." Comic creatures
were divinely designed for our merriment, and are enjoyed by
us through the gift of humor that comes from His own image

and reflects His very likeness. Zoo and circus are popular places. Helen Salisbury wrote,

> Dear God, we make You so solemn,
> So stiff and old and staid—
> How can we be so stupid
> When we look at the things You've made?
>
> How can we miss the twinkle
> That must have been in Your eye,
> When You planned the hippopotamus
> And the rhinoceros?
>
> Who watches an ostrich swallow,
> Then doubts that You like to play,
> Or questions Your sense of humor,
> Hearing a donkey bray?
>
> Could the God who made the monkey
> Have forgotten how to laugh—
> Or the One who striped the zebra
> And stretched out the giraffe?
>
> How could an oldish person
> Fashion a pelican—
> Or a perfectly sober Creator
> Ever imagine man?

Lincoln once said, "God must have meant us to laugh, else He wouldn't have made so many mules, parrots, monkeys, and human beings."

• • •

ANIMALS

A big family went for a visit to the zoo. A sign read, "Admission, $10 a family." Herding his 14 children through the gate, the father handed the ticket-collector a $10 bill.

"Are all these children yours?" the collector asked in amazement.

"Every single one of them," answered the father.

"Here's your money back," said the collector. "It's worth more for the animals to see your family than for your family to see the animals!"

• • •

An atheist was taking a walk through the woods. "What majestic trees! What powerful rivers! What beautiful animals!" he said to himself.

As he was walking alongside the river he heard a rustling in the bushes behind him. Turning, he saw a 7-foot grizzly bear charging toward him. He ran as fast as he could up the path. Looking over his shoulder, he saw that the bear was even closer. Suddenly, he tripped and fell on the ground. He rolled over to pick himself up but saw the bear right on top of him, reaching for him with his left paw and raising his right paw to strike him.

At that instant the atheist cried out, "My God!" Time stopped. The bear froze. The forest was silent. As a bright light shone on the atheist, a voice came out of the sky, "You deny my existence for all these years, teach others I don't exist, and even credit creation to cosmic accident. Do you expect me to help you out of this predicament? Am I to count you as a believer?"

The atheist looked directly into the light. "It would be hypocritical of me to ask you to treat me as a Christian now, but perhaps you could make the bear a Christian."

"Very well," said the voice.

The light went out. The sounds of the forest resumed.

And then the bear dropped his right paw, brought both paws together, and bowed his head and spoke, "Lord, bless this food which I am about to receive from Thy bounty. Amen."

• • •

Boys

A mother, concerned about her young son's potential behavior when Christian friends were coming over for the evening, asked, "Jeremy, are you going to be good when Joe and Mary come over tonight?"

Little Jeremy replied quizzically, "Are Jesus' parents coming here?"

• • •

Johnny, hospitalized, was the terror of the Children's Ward. His Sunday school teacher, who knew his mischievous nature, said, "Johnny, if you are good for a week, I'll give you a dollar when I come again."

A week later the teacher stood by Johnny's bed. "I'm not going to ask the nurse if you've behaved. You must tell me yourself. Do you deserve the dollar?"

After a short silence, a small voice from among the sheets said, "Gimme a nickel."

• • •

"Is the doctor in?" the phone caller asked.

"No, sir," answered his five-year-old son.

"Will he be back soon?"

"I have no idea," the lad replied. "He went out on an eternity case."

• • •

Little boy: "Grandpa, were you on the ark?"

Grandpa: "Of course not!"

Little boy: "Then how come you weren't drowned?"

• • •

On a Sunday during Lent a pastor invited all the boys and girls up front for the children's sermon. He began by asking a question, "Does anyone know what Lent is?"

A nine-year-old boy piped up, "It's the little specks of fluff we get on our clothes."

• • •

A physician and his family attended a church service where a report was given updating the membership list. When the secretary read off the names of those who had passed away during the year, the doctor's little boy could be heard asking in a clear voice, "Daddy, weren't all those people your patients?"

• • •

GENEALOGY

A teenager, asked about the genealogy of Jesus, replied, "Abraham begat Isaac, and Isaac begat Jacob, and Jacob begat twelve partridges."

• • •

An aristocratic southern lady was invited to a Sunday school class where the subject was Bible history. That morning the teacher centered attention on the ancient Medes and Persians, the empire that preceded the Greeks and the Romans.

After 50 minutes of what he thought was clear, acceptable instruction, the teacher was greeted at the door by the southern lady drawling, "I did so enjoy your lesson. You know—my grandmother was a Mead!"

• • •

INTEGRITY

A couple arrived late at the church for a gospel concert and found every seat had been taken. Standing at the back, they saw two people leave. When those two seats were still empty several minutes later, the couple sat down in them. The women next to the couple informed them that the seats were taken and that the folks had just left for a few minutes and would be back.

After the next hymn the song leader asked everyone to turn to their neighbors and say, "I love you."

The woman beside the couple turned and said, "I love you—but those seats are still taken."

• • •

A lady came to a stop at the red light. She was directly behind a car filled with young children, driven by their mother, and bearing a big bumper sticker, "HONK IF YOU LOVE JESUS." So the lady in the second car gave a friendly push on the horn. Whereupon the mother in the front car stuck her head out of the window, swore, and yelled, "Can't you see the light's still red?"

• • •

Before the offering a minister encouraged his congregation to "give generously, proportionately, cheerfully, in faith, and in accordance with what you reported on your IRS tax form."

• • •

A young lady was sunbathing on a beach when a little boy approached. "Do you believe in God?" he asked. The young lady replied affirmatively.

"And do you go to church every Sunday?"

"Yes, I do," replied the young lady, somewhat surprised.

"And do you read the Bible?"

"Every day," replied the young lady, becoming more interested.

Noticeably relieved, the little boy said, "Well, then will you please hold my dollar while I go swimming?"

• • •

SECRETARIES

A secretary decided to apply for work in a church office. She filled out a job application and later was interviewed by the pastor.

The pastor noted that she didn't fill in the year of her birth. "I see that your birthday is July tenth," said the pastor. "May I ask what year?"

"Every year," replied the secretary.

• • •

The Bishop acquired a new secretary, a former Pentagon employee. She immediately reorganized the diocesan filing system, labeling one cabinet SACRED and the other TOP SACRED.

• • •

Denominational executive: "My wife isn't jealous. She doesn't care how good-looking my secretary is as long as he's efficient."

• • •

Chapter 4

~ HUMOR IS SO HUMAN

It's so human to enjoy a laugh. Of all the species of creatures on earth, man is the only one who can tell or grasp a joke. Dogs cannot pose riddles to other canines, nor chuckle at the answer. TV personality Monsignor Fulton Sheen commented, "Man is the only joker in the deck of nature."[8] Without humor we are less than human.

People are funny at all ages. A baby will giggle when grandpa plays peekaboo. People are funny around the world, though what amuses one nation may not amuse another. People have been funny in all centuries. The history of humor is the history of literature. In his *Poetics*, Aristotle classified comedy as a subdivision of the tragic. Euclid framed many of his propositions in geometry with "reductio ad absurdum" type of argumentation. In the Middle Ages, Dante's famous work was called *The Divine Comedy*. The Crusades brought a flood of witty oriental tales to the west. *The Reader's Digest* over the years has received over 20 million jokes, ran more than

100,000, and paid more than $25 million for them.

Humor cannot be suppressed, and will out, sometimes in the most sober of situations. A parrot had found its way into the rafters behind the pulpit of a dignified Scotch church. Just as the minister began to preach, the parrot croaked out, "Stop yer bletherings; stop yer bletherings." Though the congregation was composed of staid Presbyterians, their humanity betrayed itself as the sound of muffled mirth first wafted through the church, then, gaining momentum, exploded into a crescendo of uncontrollable laughter.

Martin Luther enjoyed a hearty laugh when he and his wife Katie had students over for dinner where he would regale them with stories while discussing theology.

Praying Hyde, the spiritual power behind revivals in India, was known not only for the depth of his praying, but also for the hilarity of his laugh.

Oswald Chambers, author of *My Utmost for His Highest*, was also loved for his rollicking sense of humor. A serious young man, meeting Oswald for the first time, said, "I was shocked at what I then considered his undue levity. He was the most irreverent Reverend I had ever met!"[9]

Charles Swindoll suggests that when Jesus took His twelve disciples across a lake to enjoy some R&R alone on a mountainside they likely sat around a campfire, told a few jokes, and laughed.[10]

Who of us doesn't laugh at bloopers in church bulletins like, "The Apostles Greed," and "There is a Bomb in Gilead," and "The choir will sin in the evening service"? Isn't it likely that God laughs at our well-intended seriousness?

How sad to live perpetually on Lamentations Lane. So, let's do what comes naturally. Lighten up and enjoy laughter.

• • •

CHOIR

A choir director took a break during practice to explain the church calendar. He asked, "Does anyone know who decided when Lent should begin?"

A newcomer blurted out, "Hallmark!"

. . .

Choir leader: "Don't forget, choir. The sopranos will sing until we get to the River Jordan. Then when they reach the River Jordan, the rest of you will come in."

. . .

CHURCH BULLETINS

"Car engine for sale by associate pastor slightly cracked."

. . .

"Take advantage of the mobile clinic and be examined for tuberculosis and other diseases which the clinic offers free of charge."

. . .

"Several of our denomination's churches have been closed. Our leaders report that this action is necessary because of swindling congregations."

. . .

A church newsletter, reporting on the associate pastor and wife's ten-day anniversary trip: "Their two daughters were starving with relatives during their parents' absence."

. . .

"We note with regret that Mrs. Constance is recuperating from an auto accident."

. . .

"Evening massage—7 p.m."

. . .

COMMITTEES

An African in the U.S.A. for seminary training went to his first American football game. He noticed that both teams went into a huddle before every play.

"What do you think of the sport?" asked a seminary friend.

"Not a bad sport," he replied, "but they have too many committee meetings!"

• • •

One reason why the Ten Commandments are so short and to the point is that they did not come out of a committee.

• • •

Committee member: "I don't know why everyone criticizes our committee. We haven't done a thing."

• • •

A committee is an organizational device for achieving delay in an orderly way.

• • •

PRIDE

One whale to another: "Be careful out there. When you get to the top and start to blow, that's when you get harpooned."

• • •

A young man received an award from his company. The emcee used extravagant language to praise his accomplishments. Jubilantly the young man went home to show off his medal, proudly repeating the words of praise in the emcee's citation. Then he asked, "Mother, how many great men are there in the world today?"

His mother replied, "Oh, one less than you think."

• • •

TEN COMMANDMENTS

A minister was delighted at the sudden spurt of interest shown in the Bible by a young housewife who seldom came to church. She had just phoned to ask for another word for the Ten Commandments.

"Decalogue," said the pastor.

"It's so nice of you to tell me," she replied airily. "Now if the quiz program calls me today, I'm good for at least $10,000."

• • •

Lincoln, asked his opinion on a painting done by an amateur, commented, "I can truthfully say that the artist has observed the Commandments."

"How so?" asked the owner of the painting.

"Because," said Lincoln, "he hath not made to himself the likeness of anything in heaven above, or that which is on the earth beneath, or that which is in the water under the earth."

• • •

Asked what the lesson was about in Sunday school, a little fellow answered, "Today we learned about the Top Ten Commandments."

• • •

Chapter 5

MERRY MEDICINE— A WONDER DRUG

Norman Cousins, editor of the *Saturday Review* for over 30 years, is widely known because of his use of laughter to overcome an illness in which doctors gave him only one chance in 500 to live. His regimen of humor worked. In 1976 he described his brush with death in a book that found its way to the top of the *New York Times* best-seller list.[11]

Advocating the theory that laughter is good medicine, Cousins became an Adjunct Professor at the UCLA School of Medicine in Los Angeles. He was careful to point out that laughter is no cure-all, nor a substitute for competent medical care, but a part of a total strategy of treatment.

After Cousins published his story, more than 3,000 doctors sent him accounts of similar experiences. He spearheaded a growing interest in organizing joke-sharing programs to enhance the curative force of medical treatment. Organizations sprang up like "Nurses For Laughter," and hospital courses like "Humor, Hilarity, Healing, and Happy

Hypothalami."

Dr. William F. Fry, Associate Professor of Psychiatry at Stanford University Medical School in California, and long-time student of gelotology (the science of laughter), said that a person who enjoys a good belly laugh undergoes therapy in many parts of the body, a sort of "internal jogging," secreting hormones into the blood stream and giving a feeling of euphoria or "runner's high."

A doctor said, "If you can't take a joke, you'll have to take medicine." Proverbs 17:22 tells us, "A merry heart doeth good like a medicine" (KJV). Another doctor, observing that cheerful people resist disease better than glum folks, parodied, "The surly bird catches the germ." Another, "Illness is not a laughing matter. Maybe it should be." Another slogan comes from *Reader's Digest:* " Laughter, the Best Medicine."

The healing potential of humor is nothing new. Someone listed the three greatest doctors in history as "Dr. Quiet, Dr Diet, and Dr. Merryman." Medieval court jesters helped maintain the king's health. Mark Twain, in *Tom Sawyer,* tells of an old man who, after shaking with laughter from head to foot, remarked that such a laugh was money in his pocket because it cut down the doctor's bills.

A professional comedian, after successfully making his audience laugh, would report to his wife, "I killed them tonight." After learning how laughter promotes health, he told his wife, "I helped them live!"

Because merry medicine improves our health, shouldn't believers laugh more, especially since our bodies are temples of the Holy Spirit?

• • •

BANQUETS

The governor of the state was attending a banquet which he had to leave before the main course was served. The waitress brought a plate of rolls, then a pat of butter. He took a roll and buttered it. Later he reached for a second roll. When he asked for another pat of butter, the waitress refused, saying, "No, I'm sorry."

Taken aback, he said, "Do you know who I am?"

She said, "No."

He replied, "The governor of the state."

Nonplused, she asked, "Do you know who I am?"

"No," he replied.

She answered, "I'm the waitress in charge of butter."

• • •

Students entering the lunch line at Asbury Seminary saw a sign over a bowl of apples, "Take only one apple. God is watching you."

At the end of the line was a large pan of cookies beside which someone had hastily penned this message, "Take as many cookies as you want. God is watching the apples."

• • •

A wealthy widow gave a large dinner party to honor the retiring Sunday school superintendent. The guests had all been seated and had already started to eat their first course when, to her horror, the hostess realized that thanks had not been offered for the food. She apologized to the superintendent and asked for advice.

The superintendent told her not to worry. Tapping his glass to get the attention of the gathering, he proceeded to recite from the book of Psalms, "Bless the Lord, O my soul," and then, after a pause, he continued, "and all that is within me bless His holy name!"

• • •

The deacon's wife apologized to her unexpected guest for serving the apple pie without cheese. Her little boy slipped away from the table for a moment and returned with a small piece of cheese, which he laid on the guest's plate.

The visitor smiled at the lad thankfully, then remarked, "You have sharp eyes, sonny. Where did you find it?"

With a flush of pride the boy replied, "In the mousetrap."

• • •

CHURCH

As the church filled up and a crowd stood at the rear, the preacher asked, "Can those in the back hear me?"

A voice from the rear pew called out, "Yes, but I'll be glad to change with someone who can't."

• • •

Newly converted, D. L. Moody used to fill a pew in an aristocratic Boston church with street urchins. When he tried to join the church, upper-crust board members tried to discourage him. "Think it over. And pray about it too." They thought that would end the matter.

But next month a determined Moody showed up before the board again. Taken aback, the board asked, "Did you do what we suggested? Did you pray about it?"

"I did," Moody replied.

"And did the Lord give you any encouragement?"

"Yes," said Moody. "He told me not to feel bad because He too has been trying to get into this same church for the last 25 years."

• • •

Merry Medicine—a wonder drug

In mid-sermon a mother started to have a coughing spell. She usually had chewing gum handy to soothe her throat, but she had forgotten to bring any that morning. Family members sitting nearby had to stifle their laughter when her young nephew asked out loud, "Auntie, do you want me to get you a piece of gum from under this pew?"

• • •

A church's weekend crusade included a rally on a fall Sunday afternoon. The guest speaker noticed an elderly man, apparently deaf, seated near the front, listening intently through his earphones.

Suddenly, toward the end of the sermon, the voice of a football announcer interrupted the service, booming through all the church sanctuary, "The Giants are on Cleveland's 10-yard line with two minutes to go."

The earphones were not a hearing-aid, but a small radio. The elderly man had sneezed, jarring the earphones off one ear, permitting everyone to get an update on the game.

• • •

A minister complimented the parents of a baby boy who had just been christened. "I've never seen a child that has behaved so well at a christening."

The mother replied, "It's because my husband and I have been practicing on him with a watering can all week."

• • •

At the appropriate time in the service the pastor stood and said, "Let us all join in silent prayer. Please turn off your cell phones and beepers."

• • •

A megachurch, packed with worshipers for a revival service, enjoyed enthusiastic singing and dancing in the aisles. An

~ 37 ~

hour after the service ended, the sexton found a well-dressed man sprawled across three seats in the main auditorium. The sexton couldn't get him to leave, nor could the pastor. They called 911. After getting the man's name, they asked, "Where did you come from?"

He groaned, "From the balcony."

• • •

A sign over the best spot in a church parking lot:

CLERGY SPACE

YOU PARK

YOU PREACH

• • •

Hospitals

A man said, "After I was in the hospital last month, my outlook on things changed entirely. It made me really aware of the most precious things in life."

Pausing, he added, "family, friends, and hospitalization insurance."

• • •

A middle-aged man, a Sunday school teacher, entered the hospital for an operation. Before long he had a visitor who said, "Good morning, I'm Dr. Jones, and I'm going to be your surgeon. The first thing I want to know is if you're comfortable."

The patient replied, "Well, I have managed to save a little."

• • •

Old Age

An elderly lady confessed that she often thought of the hereafter. "Whenever I go to the attic, I say to myself, 'What am I up *here after?*'"

• • •

After taking a picture of a man celebrating his 95th birthday, a photographer said, "I hope I'm still around to take your picture on your 100th birthday."

Elderly man: "I don't see why you won't be. You look pretty healthy."

• • •

A reporter asked a man on his 100th birthday, "To what do you credit your long life?"

"Not sure yet," replied the old-timer. "My lawyer is negotiating at the present time with two different breakfast cereal companies."

• • •

Chapter 6

PRESCRIPTION FOR HEALTH OF SOUL

A senator remarked to Harry Truman after he left the White House, "I'm glad the President hasn't lost his sense of humor." Truman replied, "Any man who had the job I've had, and didn't have a sense of humor, wouldn't still be here."

Jim Elliot, martyred by the Aucas, wrote in his diary at Wheaton College, "God has blessed me with a queer twist that makes me laugh at almost anything. . . . Whenever I get downcast, the Lord feeds me pills of praise."[12]

A missionary suggested that folks at home should pray for a saving sense of humor for missionaries on the field. Paul Jewett observed, "A sense of humor will keep the minister and missionary more than any psychiatric therapy, for it palliates disappointments and alleviates tensions."[13]

The AARP reports that hospitals in many cities have set aside special rooms for joke-telling and laughter. Said one head nurse, "The room is an oasis."

Beatrice C. Engstrand had a cyst removed from the roof of

her mouth a year before entering medical school. But pain persisted. A year later she underwent a radical maxillectomy. The surgeon removed her left upper jaw, gum, teeth, cheekbone, and palate. In her book she describes her battle with disfigurement, frustration, and despair.[14] She became an Assistant Professor of Neurology at New York Medical College and started a private practice on Manhattan's upper east side. She tells how her mother read joke books to her in the hospital and encouraged her to laugh, even though her mouth and cheeks were immobile. The sound of Mom's laughter had eased the pain.

Interestingly, Dr. Engstrand was one of the doctors who later treated the Central Park jogger, the young Wall St. executive who had been raped, beaten unconscious, and left to die in the late 80s. Soon after the victim had been identified and her family notified, Dr. Engstrand approached the room, saw the jogger's mother standing by the bed, and identified herself as the consultant neurologist. She advised, "Don't be ashamed to laugh. Read aloud from joke books." She related how humor had helped her recover from radical surgery. The mother followed the advice, including the joke-telling.

Later the jogger came out of her coma. Through competent medical treatment she eventually recovered and returned to work.

Humor is not a cure for everything, but it is certainly therapeutic, even serving as preventive medicine. If Christians do not come apart and laugh awhile, they may just come apart. G. K. Chesterton wrote, "Madmen are always serious. They go mad from lack of humor."[15]

Lighten up. Laughter brings health to the soul.

• • •

COLLEGE

When Dr. George Sweeting retired from the presidency of Moody Bible Institute in 1987, he told the student body in chapel, "When I was in grade school, I was a champion marble player. I would come to school with a dozen marbles and go home with perhaps ten dozen marbles. Rarely did I lose, and when that happened, of course, I was finished. It's the same way with being a college president. When you've lost all your marbles, you quit."

• • •

Dennis, a basketball star at his college, was not so good at academics. At one of his exams just before Christmas he stared blankly at the questions, and grinning, wrote across the top of his paper, "Only God knows the answers. Merry Christmas."

When school resumed after the Christmas break, the hero of the basketball court found his exam paper in his mailbox, returned by his professor with the notation, "God gets an A. You get an F. Happy New Year!"

• • •

Some years ago Mohammed Ali was a graduation speaker at Harvard University. When introduced, he walked to the podium and said softly, "Go to college. Get some knowledge. Stay till you're through. If God can make penicillin out of a piece of mold, He can certainly make something out of you."

Then he returned to his seat. That was his complete speech, for which he received a several-thousand-dollar stipend.

• • •

It was graduation at a community college. Ninety-three graduates in flowing gowns and traditional caps filed into the crowded auditorium. Parents and friends smiled enthusiastically. The class had wanted a prayer in the program, but a recent court ruling prohibited it. Students were careful to stay within guidelines. Speeches were inspirational and challenging, but completely without mention of divine blessing or guidance—until the final speech and its reaction.

The last student walked with dignity to the microphone. He stood erect and quiet for a couple of seconds, then delivered his oration—an amazing SNEEZE.

Immediately the other graduates rose to their feet, and in unison they exclaimed, "God bless you!"

The audience exploded into applause. The class had found a way to invoke God's blessing with or without official approval.

• • •

Until the end of the 1930s it was compulsory at Oxford University, England, to pass a divinity course. When a star athlete entered the university, hopes ran high of winning the league rugby championship. But the student had trouble passing the Bible course. Since his presence on the team meant the difference between victory and defeat, the governing board gave him one final chance. If he could answer one question orally, all would be well for him, and for the honor of Oxford.

Standing before the board of examiners, he was asked, "Who was the first king of Israel?"

The student remained silent, and the hopes of the rugby team seemed to fade. Finally, he blurted out, "Saul."

"Absolutely correct," answered the relieved professors. "That's all we need to ask. You may leave."

At the door the athlete turned to his examiners. "But, sirs,

I should have added that it was Saul who afterwards was named Paul."

• • •

An agnostic is a guy who watches a football game between Notre Dame and Southern Methodist and doesn't care who wins.

• • •

Father: "I'm giving my son a watch for graduation."
Friend: "Is it a surprise?"
Father: "Sure is. He's expecting a sports car."

• • •

Neighbor: "Congratulations on your son's graduation from college. Must cost a bundle to send a son to college these days."
Father of football player: "Sure does. It cost me over $80,000 and all I got was a quarterback."

• • •

THE DEVIL

A young ordination candidate declared that he did not believe in a personal devil. The ministers were about to vote against him, although he had given perfectly orthodox answers in all other areas of doctrine.

Then the oldest pastor present made this comment, "Brethren, I see no reason for refusing this young man because he doesn't believe in a personal devil. He won't be pastor of a church two months before he changes his mind."

• • •

SERMONS

Just out of seminary and accepting the pastorate of a church, a young preacher proposed to the girl of his dreams.

She agreed to marry him on one condition. She wanted to keep a locked box in their closet and to have the only key in her possession. He agreed.

Thirty years went by before curiosity finally got the better of him. One afternoon when she was out shopping he, knowing where she kept the key, opened the box. Inside were three eggs—plus hundreds of $1 bills. When his wife returned home, his conscience prompted him to blurt out what he had done. She forgave him immediately. Then he asked, "Why were there three eggs in that box?"

She explained, "When we were married, I decided that every time you preached a punk sermon I would put an egg in there." He thought, "I must be a pretty good preacher—only three punk sermons in 30 years."

Then he asked, "Why all the $1 bills? Must be hundreds of them." She casually answered, "Oh, every time I sold a dozen eggs, that's where I put the money."

• • •

A minister preached a very short sermon. He explained, "My dog got into my notes and chewed them up."

At the close of the service a lady visitor made a request of the preacher as she shook hands with him at the door: "If your dog ever has pups, please let my pastor have one of them."

• • •

A lady noticed that every Monday morning her pastor drove down to a restaurant by the river where he met with three or four men. After several weeks of the same ritual, curiosity got the better of her, so she asked him what he was doing.

The pastor replied, "Those men are pastors from other churches nearby, and we've been meeting every Monday morning to exchange sermons."

"Oh, pastor," she replied, "don't do that. You always get the worst of the bargain."

• • •

At a Wheaton College (Illinois) chapel a speaker was preaching from his notes. He turned a page over when he was finished with it and let it drop over the side of the pulpit down onto the platform floor. Moments later he would release another page and so on.

Those sitting in the balcony near the front had a good view of what was happening, for they were looking right down on the pulpit.

As the preacher threw down the last page, he said, "I could go on and on. I wish I had the time to do so."

"Oh, no, you can't," came a voice from the balcony. "You just ran out of notes."

• • •

When the main preacher did not arrive before the morning service at a big camp meeting, a young pastor was asked to fill in. Scared half to death, he went to the bishop's tent. "They've asked me to preach this morning, but I don't have any sermon. What shall I do?"

"Trust the Lord, young man," the bishop said with great dignity. "Just trust the Lord." Then the bishop marched out of his tent. The young man picked up the bishop's Bible and thumbed through, hoping to find an inspiring text. He discovered some typewritten notes that he liked very much. So he took the notes and went to the service.

The young pastor's sermon amazed everybody. People crowded around after to congratulate him. Suddenly the bishop thundered, "Young man, you preached my sermon that I was going to give tonight. Now what am I going to do?"

With great dignity the young pastor replied, "Trust the Lord, bishop. Just trust the Lord."

• • •

A teenager, visiting a friend's church: "Why do you have two pulpits—one on one side, and one on the other?"

Friend: "The minister reads the Bible from one pulpit, and he preaches from the other."

Teenager: "Why is that?"

Friend: "I don't know unless it's to show that what he preaches is far removed from the Bible."

• • •

To his embarrassment a guest preacher discovered just before the sermon that his upper plate had cracked. "I'm afraid I'll have to cancel my sermon," said the preacher to the chairman.

"No need to cancel," came the reply. "Here's a spare upper plate I have in my pocket."

The guest tried it, but it didn't fit. The chairman, quick as a flash, produced another, then another, till a fourth plate fit exactly.

When the preacher finished his well-received talk, he said to the chairman, "How happy I am that you happen to be a dentist."

"Dentist? Not at all," said the chairman. "I'm a funeral director."

• • •

As the family drove home from church, their small son announced, "I'm going to be a minister when I grow up."

"Wonderful," said the mother. "What made you decide you want to be a preacher?"

"Well," said the boy thoughtfully, "I'll have to go to church on Sunday anyway. And I think it would be more fun to stand up and shout than to sit still and listen."

• • •

SAFETY VALVE

Theologian Dr. James I. Packer noted how the heavy sessions of a theological conference were punctuated by peals of laughter. For example, at one break the director casually announced that he had just met a man who had been a husband all his life. A participant, falling for the gag, said he would like to meet such a man. "Stand up, Mr. Husband," cried the director. As the man with the unlikely name stood up, the conference whooped and clapped for a full half-minute. Humor, commented Packer, provided a safety valve from the strain of the seminar.

The release of tension redeems many a social situation from unpleasantness, collapse, or disaster. When critics called attention to Ronald Reagan's age, he replied, "I will not exploit for political purposes my opponent's youth and inexperience."

One female seminarian found a handy way to respond to male students who seemed to oppose her presence or wonder why she was there. "I tell them I want to be a TV evangelist.

Chapter 7

That usually stops the questioning." Gentle humor can be the soft answer that turns away tension. A mother whose top priority was immaculate housekeeping spotted a cobweb in her married daughter's kitchen. She asked menacingly, "What's that?" Quipped her daughter, "A science project."

Someone said, "After God created the world, he made man and woman. Then, to keep the whole thing from collapsing he invented humor." Private jokes nurture the marriage relationship. One husband said, "The missus and I discovered a trick early in our marriage that has always helped us end an argument. When one gets hot-collared, the other starts barking like a dog. The first one always joins in, and each tries to make more noise than the other. We always end up laughing." A marriage generously sprinkled with humor isn't easily dissolved.

A study by an Alabama professor of family studies found a close relationship between humor and family strength. For a family, a day without a laugh may be a day that is lost.

Humor can pour oil on troubled church waters. After acrimonious debate in a business meeting, a church found itself deadlocked in a tie vote. Rather than use his constitutional prerogative to cast the deciding vote, the moderator chose to give the members time to rethink the issue. He said, "Come back next week, and we'll see if we can break the tie." He chose for the closing hymn, "Blest Be the Tie That Binds." And they laughed their way through all the verses.

Laugh more. The safety valve of humor can "untense" the intense.

• • •

DATING

A 25-year-old girl, back from a singles' retreat with a scarcity of males, was asked where she had been. Her reply,

"No man's land."

. . .

A mother, apprehensive at her daughter's first date with a new boy in the Lutheran college youth group, gave her a preview of what would likely happen. "First, he'll take you to a nice dinner. That won't worry me. Then he'll take you for a drive in his car. That won't worry me. Next he'll park at a spot with a nice view. That won't worry me. Then he'll say, 'Put your head on my shoulder.' That's when I'll worry."

Next morning, the daughter told her mother that it happened just as she predicted. "He took me to dinner, then for a ride, then parked, then said, 'Put your head on my shoulder.' But I said, 'You put your head on my shoulder, and let YOUR mother do the worrying.'"

. . .

JUDGING

Driving home late one day, a deacon picked up a hitchhiker. Growing suspicious of his passenger, the deacon checked to see if his wallet was secure in the pocket of his coat on the seat between them. But it wasn't there. Slamming on the brakes, he ordered the hitchhiker out and demanded, "Hand over my wallet!" The frightened hitchhiker handed over a billfold before the deacon drove off.

Arriving home, he started to tell his wife about the episode, but she interrupted him, "Honey, before I forget it, no doubt you know that you left your wallet at home this morning."

. . .

Six-year old Steve picked up some bad words that caused his mother anguish. On his way out to his playmate's birthday party his mother warned, "Steve, I've asked them to send you straight home the minute you use a bad word."

~ 53 ~

Fifteen minutes later Steve walked in the door. His furious mother ordered him to bed. His attempts to explain were ignored.

Later his mother mellowed. Going upstairs, she asked, "Tell me honestly, Steve, just why were you sent home? Just what did you say?"

Little Steve, humiliated but still angry, exploded, "I didn't say nuttin'. The party ain't till tomorrow."

• • •

After a concert by the Liberated Wailing Wall, a man began talking with team-member Daphne who was in charge of the sale of their CDs, as to whether he could use his credit card since he'd left his checkbook at home. Another team member was shocked when she overheard the team leader tell Daphne under his breath, "Don't give him one, Daphne; he's a sociopath."

The team member spent the rest of the evening wondering how the leader knew this about that man. Later when the team was alone, and the member repeated what he had heard the leader say, the rest of the team burst into hysterical laughter. The leader had actually said, "You can give him one, Daphne. He's the associate pastor."

• • •

MARRIAGE

Here's a story from seminary professor Dr. Ralph Keiper's courtship days. On a date with Nan he was nicely dressed, walking through a park when a pigeon let go right on his new suit. Without missing a beat Nan cleaned off the mess, commenting, "Let us thank the Lord that elephants don't fly."

Keiper, recognizing her unique sense of humor, immediately exclaimed, "Lead on, O King eternal!" And He did. They enjoyed a long, happy marriage.

• • •

Wife to marriage counselor: "We haven't agreed on a thing for six years."

Husband: "It's seven years."

• • •

A friend asked a newlywed husband, "How were your meals the first few weeks?"

The groom replied, "Not bad. After all, it takes time to find the right restaurant."

• • •

Groom: "And now, dear, that we're married, let's have a clear understanding about our affairs. Do you wish to be president or vice-president?"

Bride (sweetly): "Neither. You be both. I'll just be treasurer."

• • •

The time came in the wedding ceremony for the groom to kneel in prayer. Those who could see the bottom of his new shoes smiled. Someone had painted HELP on both soles.

• • •

NEWSPAPERS

An ad in a Saturday newspaper read: "Study the Bible with people who have as much trouble pronouncing Bible names and places as you do."

Another ad in the same paper:
ARMAGEDDON—THE EARTH'S LAST WAR
HOW AND WHERE IT WILL BE FOUGHT
AT THE FIRST BAPTIST CHURCH

• • •

A church, located in the New York metropolitan area, invited Philip Lord, then backfield coach of the New York

Laugh! 17 Reasons to Lighten Up and Laugh More

Giants' football team, to speak at a Saturday men's breakfast.

The sports section of the local newspaper captioned the article, "Lord speaks at Baptist breakfast."

• • •

A minister, speaking to the local Rotary Club, told a number of excellent, clean jokes. Noticing the reporter for the local newspaper present, the minister begged him not to report any of the jokes in his article. "You see—I plan to use them before a number of different local audiences, and I don't wish them to get around and get stale."

The reporter agreed. Picking up the newspaper the next day to read the report of his talk, the minister was startled to read, "The Reverend Jones also told several good jokes. Unfortunately, none of them can be repeated."

• • •

A Religious News release some years ago: "*Eternity* magazine will cease publishing with the January issue."

• • •

PATRIOTISM

A lady, annoyed by visits from Jehovah's Witnesses, was told that they would not pledge allegiance to the American flag and was advised to place a flag inside her front door. She did so.

Two days later she spotted a visitor coming up her walk with some literature under her arm. Ringing the doorbell, the visitor asked the lady of the house for a few minutes of her time.

The lady of the house replied, "You may have a few minutes, but first you must pledge allegiance to the flag inside the door."

The visitor pledged allegiance, then continued talking, "In all my years as an Avon lady, this is the first time I've ever been asked to pledge allegiance to the flag."

• • •

An American and a Dutchman were comparing their flags. They found them quite similar. Said the Dutchman, "You have stripes, and so do we. You have red, white, and blue, and so do we. And like you, when it gets near tax time, we feel blue. When our bill comes, we turn white. When we pay it, we see red. But in your country, you see stars too."

• • •

A father took his five-year old boy to several baseball games where "The Star-Spangled Banner" was sung before the start of every game. Then the father decided it was time for his boy to start going to church. The first Sunday was just before Independence Day. The congregation sang "The Star-Spangled Banner" at the beginning of the service. Soon as everyone sat down, the boy suddenly yelled out, "Play ball."

• • •

Chapter 8

LAUGH IT OFF

When a sparse audience showed up for one of Handel's oratorios, friends tried to console him. "Never mind," Handel joked to his friends, "the music will sound better due to the improved acoustics of an empty concert hall."

Ben Franklin said, "Trouble knocked at the door, but hearing laughter it hurried away." Finding a comic interpretation pumps air into our psychic tires to smooth our ride over the rough spots. The joy of the Lord proves to be our strength. Through our tears we smile it off. Humor has given us a "faith-lift." How often we hear, "If I didn't laugh, I'd cry."

One lady commented, "I get headaches often," then added, laughing, "but I thank God that I have a head to ache."

Serious troubles are not to be trivialized by turning them into a laughing matter. But if we learn to smile at them, life will be more bearable. Hearing that his old pastor had lost both legs to cancer, a friend decided to call him. But what would he say? A voice boomed jovially, "Shorty Sears speaking. You must have heard about my surgery. Both legs had to be amputated." The man had overcome his tragedy by giving himself a nickname that laughed at his handicap. But the victim must laugh first—before anyone else joins the laughter.

In 1994 a man living in California was heard to say, "I have now doubled my real estate portfolio. I have a south apartment and I have a north apartment." He explained, "The Los Angeles earthquake split my condo in two."

On a river patrol in Vietnam when a phosphorus grenade exploded in his hand, Dave Roever suffered third-degree burns over 40% of his upper body, and half his face was virtually burned away. As he began painful recuperation, he wondered how his wife would react to his disfigurement. (Nothing prepares loved ones for the sight of burn victims.) Brenda walked straight up to Dave's bed, and showing not the slightest tremor or shock, bent down, kissed him on what was left of his face, looked into his good eye, smiled and said, "Welcome home, Davey. I love you."

All he could reply was, "I want you to know I'm very sorry."

"Sorry for what?" she asked.

"Because I wanted to look good for you. Now I'll never look good for you again."

Grinning mischievously, she said, "Oh, Davey, you never were good-looking anyway."

That was the beginning of a deep healing that ultimately enabled him to face the world again and tell his story of marvelous recovery nationwide via pulpit, platform, TV, radio, movie and video.

Let's laugh more in the face of difficulty, because humor will help us laugh it off.

• • •

FUNERALS

After the funeral of one of his members, an Episcopal rector in Madison, Wisconsin, noted that she had left very specific instructions for her funeral service. The woman, who had never married, wrote, "There will be no male pallbearers. They wouldn't take me out when I was alive; I don't want them to take me out when I'm dead."

• • •

When the town scoundrel died, a relative offered the local preacher $1,000 if he would do the funeral and somewhere in the sermon refer to the deceased as a saint. After some deliberation the preacher agreed.

At the funeral the pastor plainly told what a scoundrel the deceased had been—alcoholic, thief, drug dealer, extortionist. Then he added, "But he has a cousin who is far worse. In fact, compared to him, he was a saint."

• • •

A minister, about to conduct an out-of-town funeral, forgot the sex of the deceased stranger, so whispered to one of the mourners in the front row, "Is this a brother or a sister?"

"Neither," replied the mourner, "only a cousin."

• • •

On his way to a burial service in the back seat of a funeral car, the pastor leaned forward and tapped the driver on the shoulder. When the driver gave a visible jump, the pastor apologized. "I didn't mean to startle you."

"That's all right, Reverend," the driver replied. "It's just that I usually drive the hearse."

• • •

A seminary student, about to conduct his first funeral, walked to the front of the funeral chapel and stood by the

Laugh! 17 Reasons to Lighten Up and Laugh More

closed casket. Turning to face the mourners, to his horror he noticed sitting directly in front of him, very much alive, the lady whose funeral he was supposed to conduct.

No one had informed him that the deceased had an identical twin.

• • •

The relative phoned the nearest florist. "The ribbon must be extra wide with 'Rest in peace' on both sides, and if there is room, 'We shall meet in heaven.'"

The florist was on vacation, and the new assistant handled the order. The floral piece caused a sensation among the mourners when it arrived at the funeral home. The ribbon was extra wide, and on it was the inscription, "Rest in peace on both sides, and if there is room, we shall meet in heaven."

• • •

New funeral director: "What magazine do you suggest I read for my occupation?"

Retiring funeral director: "Good Hearsekeeping."

• • •

PASTORS

Carol Anderson, when rector of All Saints' Church of Beverly Hills, California, was stopped in the Los Angeles International Airport by a woman unknown to her. She was not wearing her clerical garb, and the woman stared at her. "Who are you?" asked the woman.

"Why do you want to know?" replied the rector.

"I think I know you. You look familiar. Do you run a museum?"

"Well, sort of."

"Which one?"

~ 62 ~

"All Saints' Beverly Hills."

"Good heavens!" replied the woman. "You're my rector!"

• • •

A pastor, recovering in the hospital after surgery, received a get-well card from the Board of Elders. "We wish you a speedy recovery. Vote, 6 to 5."

• • •

A new couple at church, invited to the pastor's home for after-church refreshments, worried about their manners. They decided to follow the pastor's example.

The sandwiches and dessert passed smoothly. Then coffee was served. When the pastor poured some coffee from his cup into his saucer, the couple did likewise. When the pastor added sugar and cream to the saucer, so did they.

Then the pastor leaned over and gave his coffee to the cat sitting by his feet.

• • •

A preacher, known for his fast driving, had to screech to a standstill to avoid hitting another car. When the other driver stormed over to exchange words, the preacher simply handed him his card that read, "The Reverend John Brown is sorry to have missed you. He hopes to make contact with you next time."

• • •

The denomination's annual convention had just ended. A poorly paid country preacher, whose convention expenses were not subsidized by his church, paid his bill at the very fashionable headquarters hotel. He noticed a sign near the door which read, "HAVE YOU LEFT ANYTHING?"

Walking over to the manager, the preacher suggested, "That sign's wrong. It should read, 'HAVE YOU ANYTHING LEFT?'"

• • •

SCHOOL

First teacher: "Do you think we'll ever get prayer back in the public schools?"

Second teacher: "As long as there are final exams and SATs there'll always be prayer in the public schools."

• • •

A teacher reported to the principal that she had seen a group of children kneeling in a corner of the playground during the noon break. Calling the children to the office, the principal asked for an explanation.

"We were playing poker," they replied.

"Oh, I'm so relieved," sighed the principal. "I thought you were praying."

• • •

A teacher received this note: "Please excuse my son Billy's absence on Thursday as it was Ash Wednesday. (Signed) My mother."

• • •

A science teacher, sensitive to the separation of church and state issue, assigned her class "a report on any insect you choose, but please don't write about the praying mantis."

• • •

Little Johnny's mother had just presented the family with twins. The household was in a state of excitement. Father said to Johnny, "If you'll tell your teacher, I'm sure she'll give you a day off."

That afternoon Johnny came home from his Lutheran parochial school grinning from ear to ear. "I don't have to go to school tomorrow," he proudly announced.

"Did you tell your teacher about the twins?" his father asked.

"No, I just told her I had a baby sister. I'm saving the other one for next week."

• • •

Chapter 9

DEFLATING POMPOSITY

Barbara Bush never liked to be compared to Nancy Reagan. She wrote, "I hate it, because she and I are not alike, and you can't compare apples and oranges. . . . As you know, we have a lot in common. She adores her husband; I adore mine. She fights drugs; I fight illiteracy. She wears a size three; so's my leg."[16]

Humor helps humility, two words practically next to each other in the dictionary. Humor helps us take ourselves less seriously by reminding us of our fragility, our imperfections, our insignificance, and our penchant for messing things up.

Laughing at ourselves shows a degree of humility. G. K. Chesterton said, "Angels can fly because they take themselves lightly. Satan fell by force of gravity." Humor allows us to recognize and laugh at our own exaggerated self-image.

A popular English preacher came down with flu symptoms the night before he was to deliver an important sermon. Tossing in fitful sleep, he dreamed that he was in heaven and saw God pacing restlessly, wringing His hands in despair and repeating, "What am I going to do? Dick Shepherd has a cold." When he awoke, Shepherd had a good laugh over his dream, and he resumed his ministry with a reduced view of his own importance.

A college professor overheard his little girl and her neighbor playmate talking in the sandbox. "Is your daddy really a doctor?" (She had heard college students call him "Doctor.") "Yep," replied his daughter, "he's the kind of doctor that can't help anybody." The professor confesses, "When I take myself too seriously I remember that."

Humor enables us to maintain a balanced sense of our importance. The famous theologian, Karl Barth, after finishing *Church Dogmatics* in 12 volumes, jestingly imagined how this momentous work might be regarded by those with a higher view. He wrote, "The angels laugh at old Karl. They laugh at him because he tries to grasp the truth about God in a book of dogmatics. They laugh because volume follows volume, each thicker than the previous ones, and say, 'Here he comes now with his little pushcart full of volumes.'"[17]

The Scottish poet Burns said,

Oh wad [would] some Power the giftie gie [gift to give] us
To see ourselves as others see us!

Don't laugh at others; that's ridicule. Do laugh with others; that's joviality. Above all, laugh at yourself, and you'll never cease to be amused. And the more you poke fun at your own pomposity, the higher you'll grow in lowliness of spirit.

• • •

ANNOUNCEMENTS

A pastor was making the announcements in the morning service: "Tonight Bertha Belch, a missionary from Africa, will be speaking at the evening service. Come tonight and hear Bertha Belch all the way from Africa."

• • •

A pastor was telling his congregation about an important guest scheduled to preach the following Sunday. "Dr. Jeremiah James has spoken in the largest churches in the nation. To miss hearing him will be the chance of a lifetime."

• • •

A lady whose husband had just re-enlisted in the navy sent her preacher a hurried note during the church service with a request for prayer. The note said, "John Smith, having gone to sea, his wife desires the prayers of the congregation for his safety."

The minister read the note hastily. Here is how he announced the request: "John Smith, having gone to see his wife, desires the prayers of the congregation for his safety."

• • •

ATHEISTS

The new resident in the ritzy, gated boulevard didn't lose time letting people know he was an atheist and against the concept of intelligent design. Meeting a new neighbor for the first time, he would introduce himself, mention he was a research chemist, then say, "There's no need to believe in the supernatural. For example, we can make rain now. We just send a fellow up on a plane. He drops some chemicals on a cloud, and presto—it rains."

To his utter amazement one day, a neighbor's eight-year old girl piped up, "Who made the cloud?"

• • •

BIBLES

A boy, recently converted by reading the New Testament in his own dialect, came to the missionary in much distress. "Sir, my big watchdog just got hold of the Testament and tore a page out of it and chewed it up."

The missionary tried to comfort him. "We can get another Testament. Don't worry."

But the boy would not be consoled. "Think of the dog."

Supposing the boy thought the paper would do the dog harm, the missionary laughed. "If your dog can crunch an ox-bone, he isn't going to be hurt by eating a piece of paper."

"Oh, sir," cried the boy. "I was once a bad boy. If I had an enemy, I hated him and wanted to kill him. Then I got the New Testament in my heart, and I began to love everybody. Now the big hunting dog has got the book in him, and he will begin to love the lions and the tigers and won't stop them from eating the sheep and oxen!"

• • •

When a new student arrived at seminary, he noticed on the bulletin board a small sign with the simple message: "Job 7:11." At first he thought it was a Scriptural reference with a message to seminarians. But when he looked up the citation he saw it was an expression of Job's bitterness of soul. Then he thought, "How much this person must be suffering! It's someone's cry for help!"

Later he expressed his concern to the seminary chaplain who quickly answered, "Oh, that sign was on the employment board. There's a job opening at the Seven-Eleven."

• • •

One Saturday afternoon a pastor made the mistake of showing some boys the place in the Bible he was going to read in the Sunday service. When the preacher wasn't looking, the boys glued two pages together.

Next morning at the proper place in the service the pastor read aloud with dignified tone from the bottom of a page, "And Noah, when he was 120 years old, took unto himself a wife who was..." Turning the page, he continued, "300 cubits long, 50 cubits wide, and 30 cubits high, built of gopher wood, and pitched within and without with pitch."

Puzzled, he stopped. He read it a second time, ending "... 300 cubits high, built of gopher wood, and pitched within and without with pitch." He paused, then added, "Beloved, I've read through the Bible dozens of times, but this is the first time I ever saw this. But I believe the Bible to be true from cover to cover. So I accept what I read as evidence that we are fearfully and wonderfully made."

• • •

Philosopher David Hume wrote an essay on the sufficiency of the light of nature for man's spiritual need. A noted pastor, F. W. Robertson, published a sermon on the opposite thesis, pointing out that the light of nature needs to be supplemented by the light of a revelation from God.

One evening the two came together to debate the matter. At the end, when Hume rose to leave, Robertson took a light to show him the way. Hume protested, "Don't worry about me. I always find the light of nature sufficient." But opening the door, he stumbled in the dark and tumbled into the street.

Robertson jumped down beside him, and holding up his light over the prostrate philosopher to make sure he was not injured, softly but firmly said, "You need a little light from above."

• • •

FAMOUS PEOPLE

Nature lover Theodore Roosevelt used to invite naturalist William Beebe to visit him at his estate. On clear nights they would go through a ritual before retiring. They would walk on the lawn, look up and search the skies for a distant speck of light mist in a certain spot, and then one of them would recite,

"That is the Spiral Galaxy Andromeda.

It is as large as our Milky Way.

It is one of a hundred million galaxies.

It is 750,000 light-years away.

It consists of one hundred billion suns,

Each larger than our sun."

After a period of silence one of them would laughingly say, "Now I think we're small enough. Let's go to bed."

• • •

When Calvin Coolidge was president and on vacation in Vermont, he received a call in the middle of the night. A voice said, "I'm Henry Smith and I'm calling to tell you that John Jones has died."

The President replied, "What's that to me? Why do you call me in the middle of the night?"

Came the answer, "John Jones is postmaster in Burlington, Vermont."

Said the President, "I still don't see what that has to do with me."

The voice replied, "I'd like to take his place."

"It's perfectly all right with me," responded the President, "if it's all right with the undertaker."

• • •

In his early years Billy Graham was in a small town to preach. Wishing to mail a letter, he asked a little boy where the post office was. After getting directions and thanking the boy, Graham added, "If you come to church this evening, you can hear me telling everyone how to get to heaven."

"I don't think I'll bother," said the boy. "You don't even know the way to the post office."

• • •

Don Shula, widely known as the successful veteran coach of the Miami Dolphins football team, was vacationing in a remote retreat in rural Maine where he thought no one knew him. As he walked into a theater one evening, the nine people scattered around in various seats began to applaud him loudly.

Shula was surprised. Could his fame have spread so far? Sitting down, he commented to a man a few seats away, "I didn't think they knew me up here."

The man fired back, "I don't know who you are. But the owner said he wouldn't start the movie until he had ten people."

• • •

Bishop Milton Wright of the United Brethren Church led his denomination in starting Huntington College in 1890. One day he made the observation that he believed every thing that could be invented had been invented. A friend disagreed, predicting that many more inventions would come, including a machine that would fly through the air.

"Flight is reserved for angels," the Bishop replied, "and you are guilty of blasphemy."

At the time Bishop Wright had two sons living at home, Wilbur and Orville. In 1933 Huntington College awarded Orville Wright an honorary degree for inventing the flying machine with his brother.

• • •

Shortly before he was married, someone asked Abraham Lincoln about his fiancée's family.

"The Todds are very important people," Lincoln replied. "They require two 'd's' at the end of their name. The Almighty is content with one."

• • •

LIBRARY

Libraries in some colleges dislike the accounting department because of its practice of bookkeeping.

• • •

A preacher dreamed that he was in heaven and wondered if the books he had written were in heaven too. His books questioned the existence of God, the truth of the Bible, and the resurrection of Jesus. Going to the library's computer, he couldn't find any listed so he asked for the librarian's help.

The librarian asked, "What section did you look under?" The preacher replied, "Under 'Theology.'"

"Oh," said the librarian, "they've all been put under 'Fiction.'"

• • •

Librarian to the pastor: "Please do me a favor and ask that the new convert call me the 'librarian' and not the 'bookie.'"

• • •

Chapter 10

GOING FOR THE JOCULAR, NOT THE JUGULAR

When a member of the missionary committee showed up—casual and unapologetic—one hour late for an important meeting which had begun on time with every other member present, the chairman looked at his watch and gently said, "Oh, glad you could make it!" Everyone smiled. Beneath the amusing remark was a gentle reminder. Instead of a sharp rebuke, the chairman softened his point with humor.

Humor can expose the foibles of others by choosing the jocular instead of attacking the jugular. Humor becomes an awakening force, allowing the person to see his fault in an amiable, non-intimidating, non-bludgeoning way, and without loss of self-esteem. During medieval monarchies the king would often bend his ear to the court jester with his jokes and songs, while rejecting the counsel of the elite. Perhaps we should avoid a frontal, direct attack when a prophetic word would be best delivered by a jocular approach.

Journalism Professor William Zinsser calls humor "the

secret weapon of the nonfiction writer. It's secret because so few writers realize that it is often their best tool—and sometimes their only tool—-for making an important point." He cites a craze in the 60s when half the women in America were suddenly wearing hair curlers and wearing them everywhere. He tried for a year to think how to write about this phenomenon. Coming out directly and calling it an outrage or national disgrace would have been a sermon, and he knew that sermons are the death of humor. Was there not a comic way to disguise his serious point?

Zinsser hit upon an article comprised of a series of parody letters. Here's a part of one: "I have been going steady with a certain boy for two-and-a half years and he has never seen me without my rollers. The other night I took them off and we had a terrible fight. 'Your head looks small,' he told me. He called me a dwarf and said that I had misled him. How can I win him back? HEARTSICK, Speonk, New York." Zinsser says that no one who read the article could ever look at haircurlers in quite the same way. Humor caused a fresh look at something bizarre, showing that it was an outlandish practice.[18]

Spurgeon tempered criticism of his ministerial students with jocularity. Once he dismissed them for vacation saying he would like to make each one a present. "For instance, here's Smith. I'd give him a corkscrew. He has a good deal in him but it wants letting out. As for Jones, I'd give him a funnel, so he could get more in."

A joke may free a critic from the danger of severity, and thus enhance his criticism's likelihood of acceptance.

• • •

Books

A bookstore owner wired a publishing company for a

dozen copies of Dean Farrar's book *Seekers After God* to be sent at once. He received this telegram in reply, "No *Seekers After God* in Chicago or New York. Try Philadelphia."

• • •

Signs in a Christian bookstore:

"A book becomes a classic when people who haven't read it start pretending they have."

"A bookstore has its best sellers and its blest sellers."

"Some authors are luminous; others are voluminous."

"A rare book is one which a friend borrows and remembers to return."

• • •

DENOMINATIONS

The Second Ponce de Leon Baptist Church of Atlanta, Georgia, is located on Peach St. across from the Episcopal Cathedral of St. Philip. With the Episcopalians starting their Sunday morning services earlier than the Baptists, Episcopalians found it convenient to park in the Baptist lot. This prevented Baptists from parking in their own lot for Sunday school. The problem was easily solved when a Baptist deacon applied this bumper sticker to all cars parked in the Baptist lot: I'M PROUD TO BE A SOUTHERN BAPTIST.

• • •

Overheard in a post-office line:

Woman: "I'd like 100 Christmas stamps, please."

Clerk: "What denomination?"

Woman: "Has it really come to that? OK, then, I'll take 50 Protestant and 50 Catholic."

• • •

For a class assignment a boy wrote this report on the

Quakers: "Quakers are very peaceful folks. They never fight back. My father is a Quaker but my mother is not."

• • •

An Assemblies of God minister, surprised when three Episcopalian rectors he had met on the golf course walked into church, whispered to an usher, "Get three chairs for the Episcopalians." The usher didn't quite understand so the pastor repeated, "Give three chairs to the Episcopalians."

The usher, a little puzzled, stepped to the front, and assuming a pep-leader stance, yelled to an amazed congregation, "Ready, everybody! Altogether! Let's give three cheers for the Episcopalians!"

• • •

A Baptist was comparing her church with several other churches. "When it comes to dignity, we can't approach the Episcopalians," she said. "As for ritual, the Lutherans have it all over us, and in singing, the Nazarenes have us beat."

Then she added, "But when it comes to humility, we're tops!"

• • •

Asked her denomination, a little girl replied, "We go to the Resemblance of God Church on Main Street."

• • •

A California church elder told how he became a Presbyterian. Years before, when his grandmother moved from Iowa to California, a Presbyterian pastor visited her, inviting her to attend the Presbyterian church. She replied, "I'm a Baptist, and it would take an act of God to get me to change."

Just then an earthquake shook the home. Coming from Iowa, she didn't know what was happening. But when the shaking died down, she told the pastor, "I'll join."

So the elder describes himself as "a Presbyterian by earth-quake."

· · ·

DISAGREEMENTS

A nurse's aid was working in a hospital room one day when a patient knocked over a cup of water, spilling it on the floor. The patient, afraid he might slip on the water if he got out of bed, asked the nurse's aid to mop it up. The patient did-n't know the hospital's policy which said that though small spills were the responsibility of the nurse's aids, large spills were the responsibility of the hospital's housekeeping staff.

The nurse's aid decided that the spill was a large one and called housekeeping to clean it up. When housekeeping arrived, they declared the spill a small one. An argument fol-lowed over who had the responsibility for the spill. The patient listened for a few minutes, then took a pitcher of water from his nightstand and poured its entire contents on the floor and asked, "Is that a big enough puddle for you to decide who cleans it up?"

· · ·

A woman whose job was to fill requests for supplies from various store department managers was the frequent target of their abuse when their orders were neither filled immediately nor to their satisfaction. She happened to be short of stature, so when they became abusive, she would climb up on a stool she kept nearby and say, "Well, at least now we see eye to eye on this!" It never failed to break up an irate manager.

· · ·

A church's annual congregational meeting was filled with sharp disagreement. However, the final matter on the floor was non-controversial and won by a massive majority. The chairman remarked, "Your vote was much like the human face."

When the congregation looked puzzled, he explained, "The eyes (ayes) were above the nose (nos)."

The laughter dimmed the earlier dissension and sent the congregation home in good humor.

• • •

A mother dropping into the church nursery during the morning service found her five-year old son sitting in a corner on the discipline stool because he had gotten into a spitting and hair-pulling contest with another boy.

She waited till they were home before lecturing him. She asked, "Jason, have you ever seen your father and mother spit at each other?"

He said, "No, mother."

Then she asked, "Jason, have you ever seen your father and mother pull each other's hair?"

"No, mother."

Then followed a long pause, finally broken by Jason. "Mom, you ought to try it sometime. It's a lot of fun."

• • •

One Sunday a minister announced he was giving out miniature crosses. "Put this cross in the room where your family argues most. When you look at it, the cross will remind you that God is watching."

After the service the first woman out walked up to the minister and said, "I'll take six."

• • •

TOMBSTONES

Epitaph in memory of Beza Wood:

"Here lies one Wood enclosed in wood.

One wood within another.

The outer wood is very good:
We cannot praise the other."

• • •

A man had this inscription put on his wife's tombstone:
"THE LIGHT OF MY LIFE HAS GONE OUT."

Years later, after he remarried, someone wrote underneath:
"NOW HE HAS STRUCK ANOTHER MATCH."

• • •

USHERS

In church for the first time, four-year-old Johnny was given last minute orders by his eight-year-old brother. "They don't want you to talk in church."

"Who don't want you to talk?"

"The hushers. They're the ones."

"Why don't they want us to talk?"

"Because people are sleeping."

• • •

Chapter 11

THE SALT OF WIT

When Dr. Stuart Briscoe announced a sermon on the controversial film *The Last Temptation of Christ* a number of years ago, a tremendous crowd showed up. With the atmosphere tense, Briscoe thought it wise to begin by saying, "My resumes are printed just in case things go poorly." The congregation laughed. Still realizing that some there might not share his viewpoint, Briscoe, who speaks with a distinct British accent, pointed out that Pilate and the devil were the only two persons in the whole movie with British accents. He comments, "Not only do people enjoy such give-and-take, but it bonds preacher and congregation as well."[19]

People who laugh at themselves are likely to make friends more easily because they come across as warm, accepting, nonjudgmental, and inclined towards mercy. They often put speaker and hearer on common ground, setting the stage for a positive response. During the difficult early days of his first crusade in England, Billy Graham was greeted with a scattering of boos when he stood to address the student body of the prestigious London School of Economics.

Then a young man jumped to the front of the packed auditorium and began to heckle Graham, acting like an ape, gesturing, scratching, making noises like a monkey. As the students roared with laughter, it seemed that Graham had lost the crowd. But after a good laugh of his own, Graham said to the crowd, "He reminds me of my ancestors." Again the hall was filled with laughter. Then Graham added, "Of course, all my ancestors came from Britain." Another roar. All obstacles were down, and Graham was able to continue uninterrupted.

Paul may have possibly advised the use of humor in evangelism when he wrote to the Colossians, "Let your conversation be always full of grace, seasoned with salt, so that you may know how to answer everyone" (4:6). According to one authority, Greek comic writers used the verb "season" to mean "seasoning with the salt of wit."[20] The *New Jerusalem Bible* translates this verse, "Talk to them agreeably and with a flavor of wit, and try to fit your answers to the needs of each one."

One writer termed people with winsome wit, "unconscious defenders of the faith." He added that Lady Huntingdon, a wealthy countess who gave much of her wealth to Christian work, pronounced the English statesman, Sir William Wilberforce, who helped abolish slavery in Great Britain, as the "wittiest man" in the country, and the one who most attracted her to Christianity.[21]

Sanctified humor can gain a hearing for the word of God.

• • •

CHURCH BULLETINS

"Concerning our church cemetery: persons are prohibited from picking flowers from any but their own grave."

• • •

"A special meeting of the Advisory Committee will be held next Friday. Please allow two dull hours for the session."

• • •

An outside church bulletin board listed the coming Sunday morning's sermon topic: "Two Reasons Why People Are Leaving the Church." Underneath were the names of the pastor and organist.

• • •

A church bulletin contained this announcement: "There will be a prayer of blessing for expectant parents after the morning service. All expectant parents please go to the front pews and wail for the pastor."

• • •

A report on renovating the youth center read, "New windows have been installed, and the non-alcoholic bar is already plastered."

• • •

GIRLS

A little girl, removed from London during the Nazi air blitz, was going to bed for the first night away from home. She prayed the child's prayer, "Now I lay me down to sleep." When she finished, she added, "And God, please take care of yourself, because if anything happens to you, we're sunk."

• • •

When four-year-old Donna's parents visited a different church, she became excited when the candles on the altar were lit at the start of the service. In the silent prayer period that followed, she stood up on the pew and sang, "Happy birthday to you!"

• • •

In Sunday school the children were studying the parable of the prodigal son. The teacher asked, "What did the father say when he saw his son returning?"

A little girl, smiling from ear to ear, raised both tiny fists and shouted, "It's party-time!"

• • •

A mother was trying to get ketchup out of the bottle, so she kept smacking it. When the doorbell rang, her little girl greeted the minister, "Mother's in the kitchen hitting the bottle."

• • •

When a mother saw a thunderstorm forming in mid-afternoon, she worried about her little girl who would be walking home three blocks from school. Deciding to meet her, the mother saw her walking nonchalantly along, stopping to smile whenever lightning flashed.

Glimpsing her mother, the little girl ran to her, explaining enthusiastically, "All the way home, God has been taking my picture!"

• • •

A traveling evangelist, invited to dinner, was astonished to hear the young daughter of the house say that a person must be brave to go to church these days. The evangelist asked her why.

"Because," said the child, "I heard Daddy tell Mommy last Sunday that there was a big shot in the pulpit, the canon was in the vestry, the choir murdered the anthem, and the organist drowned the soloist."

• • •

A minister's daughter was put to bed early because she wasn't feeling well. "Mommy," she said, "I want to see my father."

"No, dear," replied her mother, "your father is not to be disturbed now."

Again she asked, and again received the same answer. Then the four-year-old's voice rose in volume. "Mommy," she said loudly, "I'm a sick woman, and I want my minister to visit me."

• • •

A mother had been teaching her three-year-old daughter the Lord's Prayer. After several evenings of repeating the prayer after her mother, she wanted to do it by herself. Her mother listened proudly as she clearly and carefully enunciated every phrase almost to the end of the prayer. "Lead us not into temptation," she said, "but deliver us some e-mail."

• • •

LITURGY

A catechism teacher required his class to memorize The Apostles' Creed, and to repeat it clause by clause, with each pupil having his own clause.

As the recitation began, the first boy said, "I believe in God the Father Almighty, Maker of heaven and earth." The second boy said, "and in Jesus Christ his only Son our Lord."

The recitation went on till one boy said, "From whence he shall come to judge the quick and the dead." Then silence fell, which was broken by the next boy blurting out, "Please sir, the boy who believes in the Holy Ghost is absent today."

• • •

A Lutheran pastor was scheduled to preach in a church in another state. When it came time to speak, he clipped his microphone to his lapel. Unsure as to whether it was switched on, he tapped it gently, apparently with no result. So, leaning very close to it, he said in a loud whisper that echoed across the church, "There is something wrong with this microphone."

The well-trained and responsive congregation, very familiar with the latest in liturgical language, replied at once, "And also with you."

• • •

At Sunday morning worship, a newly licensed lay reader was nervously reading the Litany in *The Book of Common Prayer* (1928 version). He besought the Lord to "eliminate" all bishops instead of to "illuminate" them.

• • •

NEW YEAR

A New Year's resolution is something that goes in one year and out the other.

• • •

Chapter 12

SUGARCOATING TRUTH

At mealtime on a flight from Hawaii to San Francisco, I heard the attendant announce, "For dinner tonight we have a choice—beef or pizza. Since the flight is full, it could be that some of you will not get your choice. But it won't matter since all airline food tastes the same." The announcement was greeted with a roar of laughter. And some passengers ate a second choice menu in a better mood.

After church a man approached Dr. Stuart Briscoe. "I've been listening to you for quite a long time now, and sometimes when I go home from church, I find a knife stuck in my ribs. I always wonder how you did that. So today I decided to watch you closely, and I found out how you did it. You got me laughing, and while I was laughing, you slipped the point home."

Humor possesses an anesthetizing effect even while piercing a hardened heart. When the ancient rabbis had a hard truth to teach the people, they would speak it with humor. Like the sugared coating of a pill, humor helps people digest solid theology.

For example, tithing is a teaching many resist. To be asked to give 10% of our income to the Lord's work goes against the grain. A pastor, teaching a new members' class on this touchy topic, began by saying, "The most sensitive nerve in the human body is the one that leads to the pocketbook." The pastor then told of a man who, in his youth, had promised the Lord a tithe of his income. His first pay was $10 a week. Promoted several times through the years, he became a top executive, earning $2000 a week.

One day he asked to see his pastor, and related how many years ago he had promised a tithe to the Lord. He asked, "How can I get released from that promise? At the start I only had to give $1 a week, but now it's $200 a week, and I just can't afford to give that much money." The old pastor looked at his friend of many years, "I'm afraid I cannot get you released from your promise. But there is something we can do. We can get right down on our knees now and ask God to shrink your income to the point where you'll only have to give $1 a week!" Humor sweetened the point.

C. S. Lewis' *Screwtape Letters*, a series of missives from Satan to one of his demons, slyly makes Christians aware of Satan's wiles and how to overcome them. The 1968 Macmillan paperback edition describes the letters as "the wittiest piece of writing the 20th century has yet produced to stimulate the ordinary man to godliness."

Humor may help make the divine message more palpable to the hearer.

• • •

ANGELS

A teenager who had just passed his driver's test was driving an elderly deacon to an evangelistic crusade in a nearby city.

Before long the youthful driver had his car hitting 75 miles an hour. The deacon leaned over, "Aren't we going a little too fast?"

"Oh, don't you believe in guardian angels?" the teenager responded. "Isn't there one out there who will take care of you?"

"Yes," replied the deacon, "but you passed him miles ago back down the highway."

• • •

CHRISTMAS

When a new child in a suburban Philadelphia Sunday school was asked in class one December where Jesus was born, he answered, "Philadelphia."

The teacher said, "No, try again."

The child said, "Pittsburgh."

When the teacher indicated another wrong answer, the boy asked, "Where was it, then?"

"Bethlehem," replied the teacher.

"Oh," retorted the child, "I knew it was somewhere in Pennsylvania."

• • •

A five-year old had one line in a Christmas pageant. Appearing in angel's garb, he was to say, "Behold, I bring you good tidings."

After practice, at home the lad asked his mother what "tidings" meant. She explained that it meant "news."

At the performance, momentarily forgetting his line, he recovered in time to shout out, "Boy, do I got good news for you!"

• • •

After the family sang some carols, four-year-old Tommy commented, "Wasn't it good of the shepherds to put on clean clothes when they went to see baby Jesus?"

Mother asked, "What do you mean?"

Johnny explained, "We just sang, 'While Shepherds Washed Their Socks by Night.'"

• • •

A little boy was playing innkeeper in a Christmas pageant. All went smoothly until the children playing Mary and Joseph reached the inn at Bethlehem.

"Do you have any room for us?" asked young Joseph.

"No, the inn is full," replied the innkeeper.

"But it's so cold outside, and my wife is going to have a baby," pleaded Joseph. "Don't you have a place for us?"

To the surprise of the director and audience, instead of showing the couple to the stable at the rear, the little boy innkeeper replied compassionately, "I'm not supposed to say this, but you come right on in."

• • •

A few days before Christmas two ladies stood looking into a department store window at a large display of the manger scene with clay figures of the baby Jesus, Mary, Joseph, the shepherds, the wise men, and the animals.

Disgustedly, one lady said, "Look at that. The church is trying to horn in on Christmas!"

• • •

One Christmas afternoon a church officer noticed that the infant Jesus was missing from the crib in the display on the church lawn. None of the church officials knew what had happened. Nor did any of the neighbors. Searchers went in all directions, but no sign of the baby.

Finally one of the searchers spied a four-year-old pulling a brand new wagon. In it was the baby Jesus missing from the church crib.

The boy explained, "I promised Jesus if I got a wagon for Christmas I would give him the first ride."

• • •

The Wise Men showed they were truly wise. Unlike most men, they were willing to stop and ask for directions.

• • •

MONEY

St. Patrick's Day: "the wearin' of the green."
April 15 (IRS due date): "the sharin' of the green."

• • •

The chairman of the Finance Committee circulated this note among the other members of the board: "Next Sunday morning the following trustees are designated to count the offering: Robb, Crook, and Cheatham."

• • •

A little girl, raising money for her church club, asked to see the manager of a large office. Ushered into his office, she asked if he would make a contribution.

With a smile he placed a dollar bill and a dime on his desk, and said, "Take whichever you want."

The child replied, "My father always taught me to take the smallest, but I'll need the green piece of paper to wrap it in so I won't lose it."

• • •

A minister was known for his ability to take big offerings. To the amusement of other parishioners, a lady in the congregation had difficulty pronouncing the word "Reverend," and always introduced him to others as Revenue Smith.

• • •

A Sunday school teacher was explaining the difference between an offering and a collection. He told about a boy whose mother served a chicken dinner. The boy sneaked some good meat on a plate for his dog, first a leg, then a wing, then some white meat. His mother spotted the plate. "Oh, no, you don't." She made the boy put back the meat, then after the meal gave him a dish of bones for Towser.

As the boy put the bones down in front of the dog, he said, "I did have an offering for you. Now its only a collection."

• • •

A little boy fumbled around noisily in his pocket at offering time. His irritated mother whispered, "Whatever are you looking for? You already have your quarter in your hand."

"I'm looking for another quarter," said the lad. "If God is as good as the man on the platform says, then I'm raising his allowance."

• • •

SUNDAY SCHOOL

Returning from Sunday school, a boy proudly announced to his parents that he had been asked to read from the Bible in class that morning. Asked what passage, he replied, "The gossip according to John."

• • •

A Sunday school teacher related the story of the Good Samaritan. Then she had the class role-play the parable. They reached the place where the Good Samaritan came upon the beaten man by the side of the road and cried out, "Oh, no! This man is beaten and robbed. What shall I do?"

From the back of the room a very intent child yelled back, "Call 911!"

• • •

Explaining the various items in the Christian's armor, a Sunday school teacher said, "Another weapon we should carry is the Word of God. Can anyone remember what the apostle Paul called the Word of God?"

When no answer was forthcoming, he added, "It's very sharp, something that cuts."

One little fellow jumped up, "I know. It's the axe of the apostles."

• • •

Chapter 13

PUNS IN THE BIBLE

Sixty guests attended the first Chicago-area dinner of Save the Pun Foundation in 1986. One guest, an actor who hobbled in with a broken foot, commented, "This is the first time I've spent 10 weeks in the same cast," adding, "I asked the doctor for painkillers, but they were all in vein." Speaker of the evening, Harvey C. Gordon, wrote a pun book, *PUNishment.* When rejected by 80 publishers, he formed his own Punster Press—and sold 125,000 copies.

Many are surprised to learn that the Bible contains numerous puns. Old Testament Professor Dr. Arthur B. Fowler wrote, "There are scores of plays on words in the Bible. If you are at home in the Hebrew Bible, you will find it 'full' of lovely tricks of Hebrew expression."[22]

For example, when Abraham and Sarah were very old, God revealed that Sarah would bear a son. On hearing this ludicrous news Abraham fell to the ground in a spell of laughter (Gen. 17:17). Perhaps it was the most preposterous joke he had heard in his nearly 100 years of life. Then God told them to name their son, "Isaac," which means "he laughs"(Gen. 17:19).

After Samson's slaughter of a thousand Philistines he exclaimed, "With the jawbone of an ass heaps upon heaps . . . have I slain a thousand men" (Judg. 15:16, KJV). Samson celebrated his victory by a play on words—the original words for 'ass' and 'heaps' being nearly the same.[23] Moffat, to save the pun in English, translates, "And Samson said, with the jawbone of an ass, I have piled them in a mass."

Because of the many plays on words in Pauline epistles, it has been suggested that "Perhaps Paul gave the pun canonical stature."[24] Paul tells the Thessalonians that "there are some which walk among you disorderly, working not at all, but are busybodies" (2 Thes. 3:11). The words "working" and "busybodies" in Greek are participles from the same verb, except that the second verb has a prefix to make it intensive—"working at nothing." It could be paraphrased, "Some are idle, working not, but yet are working hard, officiously bustling in other people's affairs." Other translations are "busybodies instead of busy."

Sending a converted runaway slave, Onesimus (which means "profitable"), back to his master would profit Philemon. Master Philemon's forgiveness of Onesimus would bring profit (Philem. 20) or payback to Paul from Philemon, who, as Paul reminds him, is certainly in debt to the apostle for his part in sending him back. This play on words brings a delicate touch to Paul's plea.

The Bible makes generous use of the practice of punning. Should we not enjoy this form of humor?

• • •

BIBLES

A collector of old books ran into a friend who said he had just thrown away an old Bible that had been in the family for generations. "Somebody named Guten something or other had printed it."

"Not Gutenberg!" gasped the book collector. "You threw away one of the first books ever printed. A copy sold for over $400,000 last month!"

The friend explained, "My copy wouldn't have brought a dime. You see—some fellow by the name of Martin Luther had scribbled his name on it."

• • •

Though a pastor who once served a deaf congregation had a good background in sign language, he never did learn the sign for "testament," so each week he would spell "Old Testament" and "New Testament" letter by letter.

One Sunday he decided to be inventive. He made the sign for "old," and then the sign for the letter "T." The congregation giggled. When he followed the same procedure for "New Testament" again the congregation giggled.

After the service one of the congregants, still giggling, asked, "Do you know what you read today? You read lessons from the old and new toilet."

• • •

HYMNS

The pastor and song leader of a church were having a conflict over the choice of hymns. The pastor complained that the hymns too often didn't fit the theme of the service, or were not familiar and poorly sung. Most everyone noticed one Sunday when after the pastor's sermon on "The Sin of Gossiping" the song leader selected "I Love to Tell the Story."

The following Sunday the pastor told the congregation that if things didn't change, he was considering resignation. The congregation gasped when the song leader led them in "Why Not Tonight?"

No one seemed surprised when a week later the pastor announced his resignation. He explained that Jesus had led him there, and now was leading him away. The song leader couldn't resist, "What a Friend We Have in Jesus."

• • •

The congregation couldn't refrain from a few smiles and giggles when a young, very pregnant woman rose in the choir and sang, "O Lord, make haste and deliver me."

• • •

An overnight guest in the home of a young couple was awakened by a voice singing, "Nearer, My God, to Thee." At breakfast the guest mentioned how delighted he was to hear that lovely old hymn so early in the morning, but that he had never heard it sung that fast.

"Oh," replied the hostess, "I wasn't paying attention to what I was singing. You see—it's a hymn my mother used to sing. And I found that it's a good one to boil eggs by. I repeat the first verse five times rapidly for soft-boiled, and eight times for hard."

• • •

Missions

A cat chased a mouse into an underground sewer. From its hiding place the mouse listened nervously wondering where the cat was. Just then the mouse heard a dog bark. Knowing that cats fear dogs, the mouse thought it was safe to come out. The minute it did, the cat pounced on the mouse who then realized that it was the cat that had barked.

"Before you have your meal," the mouse begged the cat, "grant me this one request. Why did you learn to bark?"

Replied the cat, "To survive in this global world, you have to be bilingual."

• • •

A missionary was suddenly surrounded by hostile-looking tribesmen in a South American jungle. Noting their poised spears and poisoned arrows, he knew he had to think of something quickly. Fortunately he had a working knowledge of their language.

At that moment a plane flew overhead. "See that bird up there?" said the missionary. "That's my friend. If you hurt me, that bird will hurt you!"

The chief took one glance at the sky, then answered, "That's no bird. That's a Boeing 747!"

• • •

A missionary gave an impassioned plea for young people to consider service on the mission field when they chose their life vocations. After the service a junior in high school approached the missionary. "I think I can guess what you want," said the missionary. "You want to be a missionary when you grow up, don't you?"

"Oh, no, sir," answered the junior. "I just wondered if you had any foreign stamps you could give me."

• • •

A college student at a banquet sat next to a stranger, an African, and wondered how he would communicate with him. When the coffee came, he said to him, "Yum, yum—good, eh?" To his amazement, the African was called up as the speaker for the occasion. Converted through missionaries, educated at Oxford, he spoke in flawless English.

He returned to his seat midst great applause, turned to the American and said, "Blah, blah, blah—good, eh?"

• • •

At an airport a mother was seeing her daughter off to join a group headed for a summer short-term missions assignment in Mexico. Learning that her daughter's flight might be diverted, and that her daughter had very little change with her, the mother gave her a credit card and every bit of change she had.

Walking away after her daughter's plane left, the mother lamented to herself how traveling youth had such little foresight. And she congratulated herself on her own ability to anticipate her daughter's possible predicament.

But her smugness rapidly dissipated when she got in her car and drove up to the parking lot's tollbooth.

• • •

THE TONGUE

A first-year seminary student, sitting down in church one Sunday morning and noticing that the guest preacher was one of his professors known for his dullness, muttered out loud, "Oh, no!"

Sitting beside a lady he didn't know, he felt he should explain. "That's Mr. Dry up there. He's my professor at seminary. I had him three days this week, and now this'll be the fourth time. He's so dry!"

A smile came across her face. She asked, "Do you know who I am?"

"No."

"I am Mrs. Dry, wife of your professor."

The student asked, "Do you know who I am?"

She replied, "No."

He exclaimed, "Praise the Lord!"

• • •

"My talent is to speak my mind," said a hotheaded woman to John Wesley.

Wesley replied, "My dear woman, God wouldn't care a bit if you buried that talent!"

• • •

"A dog has many friends because he wags his tail instead of his tongue."

• • •

"A person with the gift of gab should not forget to wrap it up."

• • •

"Nothing irritates us more than to have someone go right on talking when we are interrupting."

• • •

Known to be the worst gossip in the community, a lady came up to the front of the church at the end of a service and said to the pastor, "I'd like to lay my tongue on the altar."

Replied the pastor, "I'd like to help you but the altar is only 15 feet long."

• • •

Four preachers began discussing their own weaknesses. Said the first, "I must confess that I myself am not perfect. In my younger years I swore like a trooper. Even now at times I find myself using profane language."

Said the second, "My recurring fault is alcohol. Of course, I imbibe very infrequently, but at times I am tempted beyond my powers."

The third, whispering in seeming shame, "I 'fess up to looking at pornography."

"Well, gentlemen," said the fourth, "my besetting vice is gossip and I can hardly wait to get out of here!"

• • •

Chapter 14

HUMOR IN THE BIBLE

The Bible is not a joke book. However, humor of every kind is present, and in quantity, but not always recognizable because what is funny in one language, culture or generation may not be in another. A three-day conference in Turin, Italy, in February 2005 on *Laughter and Comedy in Ancient Christianity* insisted that the Old and New Testaments are riddled with humor and clever wordplay.[25]

By associating incongruous items the book of Proverbs conveys moral truth in a pithy and often humorous way. We would grin if we saw a gold ring hanging from a pig's nose. "Like a gold ring in a swine's snout is a beautiful woman who shows no discretion" (11:22). Beautiful, but dumb!

Irony involves an intended meaning opposite to the sense of the words used. When Job called his friends "comforters" (16:2), he meant that they were anything but comforting. "Job's comforters" has become an expression to describe those who, under the guise of comforting, make you miserable. The prophets especially employ irony freely to convince the people of the folly of trusting in idols which cannot see, hear, speak, or pick themselves up.

We are amused reading of Jacob, who, after working seven years for Rachel, finds out that he was given her older sister, Leah, as his wife by their father Laban (Gen. 29:18-25). We smile at short Zacchaeus, chief tax-collector of Jericho, climbing a tree to glimpse Jesus as he passes by.

When Peter, miraculously released from prison, hurried to the home where the church was praying, is it not funny that the servant girl Rhoda rushed inside with the news, leaving Peter standing outside in danger? How laughable that the believers thought it couldn't be Peter, but his ghost, when all that night they had been praying for his release (Acts 12:1-16).

Many a preacher has derived a sneaky sense of gratification in recalling that someone fell asleep while the great apostle Paul was preaching. During his lengthy sermon at Troas a young man entered "the land of Nod" and fell quite a distance from an upstairs window to the ground, but miraculously was unhurt (Acts 20:9-11). Long sermons, and people sleeping in church, are frequent targets of jokes, like the pastor who warned his congregation not to snore lest they wake the deacons. The name of the youth that fell asleep was for years the title of *Christianity Today*'s popular humor column—*Eutychus*.

The wide presence of humor in the Bible makes the practice and enjoyment of laughter seem reasonable.

• • •

FATHERS

Two viewpoints on Father's Day:

Small boy's definition: "Just like Mother's Day, only you

don't spend as much."

Father's comment: "What I get for Father's Day are the bills from Mother's Day."

• • •

A little boy ran in from play to the living room one evening where his father was reading the newspaper. "Dad, where did I come from?"

Mother cleared her throat and excused herself, leaving the room to let Father answer this long-feared question. Father cleared his throat and went through a long, careful explanation of how babies are born.

When he was finally through, junior said, "That's okay, dad, but my pal Joe down the street says he came from Chicago, and I just wanted to know where I came from."

• • •

A father was posing at Christmas time with his college son. When the photographer suggested that the lad stand with his hand on his father's shoulder, the father replied, "It would look more natural if he could place his hand on my pocket."

• • •

A sixth-grader walked up to his father and said, "Dad, here's my report card and here also is an old one of yours I found in the attic."

• • •

A little boy looked up at his father and asked, "Before you married mom, who told you how to drive?"

• • •

When a longhaired teenager asked his father if he could use the car, his father replied, "I already told you. No haircut— no car."

The son retorted, "But dad, Jesus had long hair."
The father added, "And Jesus usually walked."

• • •

INTRODUCTIONS

A distinguished educator was introducing Leighton Ford, Billy Graham's brother-in-law, as guest speaker at a college chapel. He began, "Perhaps some of you don't know that Leighton Ford is married to Billy Graham's brother."

Unaware of his error and puzzled by the students tittering, the educator added, "That makes Leighton Billy Graham's son-in-law." The students roared.

The usually meticulous leader only added to the comedy of errors by concluding, "So now I present to you Leighton Ford's brother-in-law, Billy Graham!"

• • •

When it came time for the keynote address, the convention chairman rose to say, "Unfortunately our speaker who was scheduled to address us tonight on the topic, 'How To Solve World Problems,' was unable to make it. He couldn't find a babysitter."

• • •

At the church's annual dinner, as time neared for the message, the emcee turned to the guest preacher and asked, "Shall we let the crowd enjoy themselves a little longer, or shall we have your sermon now?"

• • •

A guest preacher at a New York City church, who had graduated from Penn State and who was staying at Park Central, was introduced by the pastor as coming from the state pen, and sleeping in Central Park.

• • •

LYING

A small country church had just concluded a week of revival services and was having a baptismal service in a river on a cold January day. The preacher asked one baptismal candidate, "Is the water cold?"

"Naw!" he replied.

Someone shouted, "Dip him again, pastor! He's lying!"

• • •

MARRIAGE

A young couple came into the pastor's office to fill out the pre-wedding questionnaire. The young man was quite nervous. When he came to the question, "Are you entering the marriage of your own free choice?" there was an awkward pause.

Finally, his fiancée looked at the young man and said, "Put down 'yes.'"

• • •

Telegram to newlyweds: MAY YOU HAVE THE WISDOM OF SOLOMON, THE PATIENCE OF JOB, AND THE CHILDREN OF ISRAEL.

• • •

An elder, returning from work one day, found his little boy and little girl quarreling rather violently with each other. When it looked as if they were coming to blows, he stepped in and asked, "Children, why are you fighting?"

The little lad answered with an airy smile, "Why, daddy, we weren't really quarrelling. We're just playing mommy and daddy."

• • •

A boy attended his first wedding. Later his cousin asked, "How many times can a man marry?"

"Sixteen," the boy responded. His cousin was amazed at his quick answer. "How do you know that?"

"Easy," the little boy said. "All you have to do is add it up. Like the preacher said—four better, four worse, four richer, four poorer."

• • •

In Vermont, a farmer used to sit on the porch with his wife. One day he began to realize how much she meant to him. It was about time for they had been married 42 years, and she had been a hard worker.

After awhile, as they sat together, he said, "Wife, you've been such a wonderful woman there are times I can hardly keep from telling you."

• • •

A man had his credit card stolen on a trip to Hawaii. When a couple of months went by, his friends wondered why he hadn't reported his loss.

He explained, "I find the thief is charging far less on my card than my wife ever did."

• • •

Chapter 15

THE HUMOR OF JESUS

That Jesus used humor may come as a surprise to some. Sad saints remind us that nowhere in the Gospels do we have any record of Jesus laughing or smiling. Is He not called "Man of Sorrows?" On the other hand, the Gospels picture Him as cheery, and entering into the good times of people. Basically, He was a Man of Joy, and wished that His joy would be ours. He was invited to a wedding, not for His sad face, but because He was a delight to be around.

A divinity school dean wrote, "For Jesus, puns, jabs, and jokes are sacred teaching tools. . . . Jesus founded the church on a pun: Matthew 16:18 reads, 'You are (Petros), and on this (Petra) I will build my church.' For a church built on a pun to be uneasy around laughter is ironic."[26]

Henri Cormier, a French priest, wrote a book *The Humor of Jesus,* which lists 60 instances of His humor.[27] For example, Simon was impetuous and oscillating, blowing hot and cold in the same breath. He dared to walk on water, then began to sink. He boasted he would never deny Jesus, but later denied Him three times. Yet when Jesus first met Simon, He called him Peter (rock). That was like calling a dwarf "Goliath."

Though Jesus saw Simon for what he would ultimately become, Simon's friends probably snickered.

Warning against unjust judgment of another, Jesus pictured a man with a plank in his eye criticizing a person with a speck in his eye (Matt. 7:3-5). To update the story, imagine a man with a telephone pole protruding from his eye criticizing another man with a sliver in his.

His listeners must have laughed at His mention of a man diligently straining out an insect from his cup, yet swallowing a camel, hump, legs, and all (Matt. 23:24).

Jesus used humorous images to poke fun at Pharisaical hypocrisy, like the portrait of a guest haughtily sitting at the head table at a banquet, then a few moments later being publicly ushered to a much inferior table (Lk. 14:7-11).

On the first Easter morn, two disciples walking the Emmaus road are joined by a stranger who asks the topic of their lively conversation. How funny that the very person they have been discussing stands there unrecognized, and then walks miles with them, explaining Scripture, still unrecognized, till He makes Himself known in their home (Lk. 24:13-35). G. Campbell Morgan said, "There's a tender playfulness in the way He dealt with these men. I cannot study the life of Jesus without finding humor there."[28]

If Jesus used and enjoyed humor, why not us?

• • •

DENOMINATIONS

A trucker wanted to drive a huge trailer out of New York City when traffic would be lightest. A policeman advised him that at 8 a.m. Sunday mornings Catholics would be at mass, Protestants sleeping since their services were usually later, and Jews out of town after their Saturday Sabbath.

So the trucker left Sunday morning at 8. As he drove out of the Lincoln Tunnel, he was struck from behind by a Seventh Day Adventist.

• • •

Six men were marooned on an island, two Catholic, two Jewish, and two Baptist.

The two Catholics started the Church of the Sacred Heart.

The two Jews started the Reformed Temple.

The two Baptists started the First Baptist Church and the Second Baptist Church.

• • •

In a city-wide revival campaign, the presiding chairman, an enthusiastic Southern Baptist, asked the congregation, "How many of you are Southern Baptists? Please stand."

One of the few who failed to rise was a little old lady near the front. "Lady, what are you?" asked the leader.

"I'm a Presbyterian," she meekly answered.

"Why are you a Presbyterian?" continued the leader.

"Well," replied the little old lady hesitatingly, "my grandmother was a Presbyterian, my father was a Presbyterian, and my husband was a Presbyterian."

"Suppose," roared the leader, "that your grandfather and father and all your relatives had been morons, what would that have made you?"

"Oh, I see," she said thoughtfully. "I would have been a Southern Baptist."

• • •

Two ministers, each convinced of his own denomination's superiority in doing things, were engaged in good-natured conversation.

"Who's to really say which is better?" commented one.

"You're right," said the other with a twinkle in his eye. "You do God's work in your way, and I in His."

• • •

A Presbyterian family had a death while their minister was away. When the local Methodist minister was asked to conduct the funeral service, he said he would have to clear it with his bishop.

Back came the bishop's e-mail, "Sure, bury all the Presbyterians you can."

• • •

The masked bandit lined up all the customers against the wall of the bank, then went from one to the other, demanding their money. Finally, the last man in line said, "You wouldn't rob a minister, would you?"

"Which church do you preach in?" asked the bandit.

"I'm a Baptist."

Placing his gun in his left hand, the bandit stuck out his right hand. "Put it there, brother. I'm Baptist too."

• • •

A member of the Plymouth Brethren lost his leg in an accident. Rushed to a Congregational hospital, he was operated on by an Episcopal surgeon, and cared for by a Presbyterian nurse. He then advertised for a wooden leg in a Disciples' paper. A Methodist widow, whose handicapped husband had been a Baptist, took his artificial leg out of storage and sent it to this needy believer. When the amputee learned the full story, he sighed, "I guess I'm a United Brethren."

• • •

PASTORS

A bishop arrived at a cathedral in a large city. The bell was rung three times. The bishop asked why.

Came the answer. "For an ordinary pastor we ring the bell one time. For an archbishop or district superintendent, two times. But for a bishop or any other kind of calamity, three times."

• • •

At a church social a visitor asked the pastor to guess her age. When he hesitated she said, "Oh, you must have some idea."

"I have two ideas," he admitted. "My problem is—I can't decide whether to make you ten years younger because of your looks, or ten years older because of your wisdom."

• • •

After the birth of their child, a Lutheran pastor, wearing ecclesiastical garb, visited his wife in the hospital. He greeted her with a hug and kiss, and gave her another hug and kiss when he left.

Later the wife's roommate commented, "My, but your pastor is sure friendlier than mine."

• • •

A pastor with lots of problems and pressures was asked how he slept. He answered, "I sleep like a baby. I sleep an hour, then I wake up and cry the rest of the night."

• • •

Little boy: "Mom, why does the pastor get a month's vacation when daddy only gets two weeks?"

Mom: "Well, son, if he's a good pastor he needs it. If he isn't, the congregation needs it."

• • •

A Welsh preacher was candidating in an English church, hoping to receive a call to be their next pastor. In the sermon, wishing to make an impression, he said, "This verse in the New Testament goes like this in the original language." Then he talked in Welsh, which sounded very scholarly to the congregation. The preacher noticed a man on the back row laughing as though his sides would split. Continuing in Welsh, he added, "Thou jolly old Welshman, I pray thee, do not give me away."

• • •

PREACHERS' WIVES

A preacher in the habit of exaggerating said to his wife on their way to church, "If I start exaggerating this morning, please make a sign and I'll stop." In the sermon he began to tell about a big church he had visited as a boy. "It was 900 feet long, 300 feet wide, and. . ."

Just then his wife gave him the sign. So he meekly ended his description, "Of course, it was just 6 inches high."

• • •

A young pastor and his wife were spending a few days at their denominational annual convention in a big city hotel. Just before retiring the first night, the wife said, "I'm a little leery. This place could be bugged."

Her husband replied, "Oh, it's perfectly safe." But she insisted that he do a little investigation. Sure enough, he discovered a lump in the carpet under the bed. So he got hold of a screwdriver and unfastened the little gadget.

Next morning the front office phoned to ask if they spent a good night. They assured the woman at the desk that it had been a most pleasant night. Then the woman on the phone mentioned that the room below theirs had reported that a chandelier had fallen to the floor.

• • •

A pastor said that when he was courting his wife, he took her to an expensive restaurant. She looked over the menu and said, "Guess I'll have the steak and lobster."

He said, "Guess again."

• • •

A newly married pastor told his wife that he had to go to New York for a committee meeting and would be gone for four days, adding, "I hope you won't miss me too much."

"I won't," answered his young wife, "because I'm going with you."

"I wish you could, but I'm going to be too busy to be with you. Why do you want to go?"

"Because I need clothes."

"But darling, you can get all the clothes you want right here in the local mall."

"Thank you. That's all I wanted to hear."

• • •

Chapter 16

HE WHO LAUGHS LAST

A couple, college sweethearts who had gone separate ways and whose mates had died, were reunited after 60 years. The old spark was still there. After two dates he fell to his knees and said, "Honey, I have two questions. First, will you marry me?"

Immediately she said, "Yes. What's the second question?"

Came his reply, "Will you please help me up?"

As we get older, we need more and more help. A greeting card said on its cover, "Old age is in your head." Inside it added, "and in your back, knees, kidneys."

In an interview of a Hawaiian lady celebrating her 118th birthday, she was asked the secret of her long life. She answered, "a sense of humor." Then she added, "I believe I'll die laughing." Laughing contributes both to longevity and to quality of life in the elderly.

Dr. Sherwood Wirt, first editor of *Decision* magazine, wrote in his book *I Don't Know What Old Is, But Old Is Older*

Than Me, "I intend to laugh all the way to heaven. I'm happier now than I ever was." He has helped seniors live richer and happier lives. Vision and faith are needed. So many "chronologically disadvantaged" have done wonderful things. To name a few, at 100 years Grandma Moses was still painting pictures. Michelangelo was designing churches at 88. Thomas Edison invented the telephone at 84. Asked why he had taken up the study of Greek at 94, Supreme Court Justice Oliver Wendell Holmes replied, "Why, my good sir, it's now or never."

Pondering our home above is helpful. Heaven is beyond description. An old saint, reclining in a lawn chair one evening and looking up at the star-studded sky, exclaimed, "If the wrong side of heaven is so beautiful, what must the right side be like?"

A Christian lady, terminally ill in midlife, bravely picked out her gravesite just two weeks before she died. After the graveside service the cemetery manager who had helped her select the spot, remarked, "Only two weeks ago I showed her another plot nearer the highway. I'll never forget her words as she turned down my suggestion. She said, 'The fumes would kill me.'" He was much impressed with her faith in the risen Christ that allowed a sense of humor to help her face an imminent death.

An eight-year old girl, on learning that her grandmother had died after suffering 15 years with Alzheimer's Disease, exclaimed, "Well, praise the Lord. Grandma's in heaven and now she knows everybody."

• • •

MISSIONS

Airline policy required its pilots to greet passengers as they exited the plane to thank them for flying with their airline. The pilot stood at the door uneasily, certain somebody would have a comment after his rough landing. Finally, everyone had passed by without remark except for one fragile grandmother who smiled and said, "Sonny, I want to ask you a question. Did we land, or were we shot down?"

• • •

Dr. Myron Cedarholm, a Baptist leader from America, was visiting his denomination's missionary station in India. Invited to speak to the national believers, the visiting executive told of headquarters operations back in the USA, rattling off the latest figures and meaningless statistics. The veteran missionary who was translating, Dr. Eric Frykenberg, sensed that the nationals had no interest in what the American was saying.

Ten minutes later, while the visitor was still spewing out statistics, some nationals began to come forward. The flustered speaker asked Dr. Frykenberg why people were coming up front.

The missionary replied, "When you started to talk about your headquarters' operations back in America, I began to preach an evangelistic sermon, and I just gave an invitation!"

• • •

A young missionary candidate met his wife-to-be during missionary training. Then they were given assignments on different sides of the world. For two years they kept the long-distance relationship alive by correspondence. Toward the end of their terms he popped the question, and she accepted.

He wrote her father whom he had never met, "I would like permission to marry your daughter and for your blessing on the marriage."

His response: "You have my permission and my blessing, but remember, there is no refund on mail-order brides."

• • •

An international airline once had an ad that read, "Breakfast in London. Lunch in New York." A missionary, who recently had experienced an unfortunate incident, felt like scribbling underneath one of these ads, "and baggage in Bermuda."

• • •

OLD AGE

The 98-year-old Mother Superior from Ireland was dying. The nuns were gathered around her, trying to make her last moments as comfortable as possible. They gave her some warm milk, but she refused.

Then a nun recalled a bottle of Irish whisky received as a gift the previous Christmas, and taking the glass back to the kitchen, she opened the bottle and poured a generous amount of the whisky into the warm milk. Back at the Mother Superior's bed, she held the glass to her lips. Mother sipped a little, then a little more, and before they realized it, she had drunk the whole glass down to the last drop.

With great earnestness the nuns asked, "Mother, please give us some wisdom before you die."

She raised herself up in bed and with a pious look on her peaceful face said, "Don't sell that cow."

• • •

"Who's absent-minded now?" the old deacon gleefully asked his wife as they walked from church. "You just left your umbrella in the rack, but I remembered both mine and yours." He proudly showed her the two umbrellas.

"But," said his wife, "neither of us brought an umbrella today."

• • •

Said a senior citizen, "I know why they call them the golden years—you get the years and the doctors get the gold."

• • •

At a luncheon for church seniors, a 101-year-old lady, asked if she had any worries, replied, "Not since I got my eldest son into an old people's home."

• • •

At age 20 we worry about what others think of us.

At age 40 we don't care what they think of us.

At age 60 we discover they haven't been thinking of us at all.

• • •

SEMINARIES

In the seminary class "Practice Preaching," each student had to deliver three sermons during the semester, all written in full. One student with a fair amount of cash but not a clear call to the ministry, secured the services of an unprincipled student to write out these sermons for him. The first two were so well written that the entire seminary faculty decided to attend his third sermon.

A few days before the delivery date the seminary student for some reason lost his temper and poured abuse on the student ghostwriter. On the day of his third sermon the seminarian began to preach, reading the first five pages in booming tone. But when he turned to page six, he found only these words in large letters, "From now on, meanie, you're on your own."

• • •

A seasoned pastor, lecturing at a seminary, advised, "If you ever forget the marriage ceremony in the middle of a wedding, start quoting Bible verses till you remember."

Next Saturday one of the seminarians was performing his first wedding. Sure enough he forgot what came next. So, he blurted out the only Scripture that came to mind, "Father, forgive them, for they know not what they do."

• • •

A seminary student pursued a rigorous course of learning. After earning his M.Div. degree, he acquired an M.A. in Philosophy, and then his Ph.D.

Collapsing under the strain, he paid a visit to his physician who gave this diagnosis: "You are killing yourself by degrees."

• • •

A homiletics student asked his professor if a good beginning and a good ending were the makings of a good sermon.

"Yes," the professor replied, "if they come close enough together."

• • •

Two old saints were discussing a sermon just delivered by a student from seminary.

"I thought it was divine," said the first. "It reminded me of the peace of God. It passed all understanding."

"Funny, I thought it was divine too," said the other, "only it reminded me of the mercy of God. I thought it would endure forever."

• • •

A seminary student on his first Sunday in his first church, wishing to make a good impression, arrived early to see that everything was in order. Noticing a dog in the aisle, he chased the animal out. It made a yelp as it scampered out the door.

After the sermon an elder said, "You may as well pack up."

"Why," asked the new pastor.

"That dog you chased out belongs to the senior trustee."

Hurrying to the senior trustee's home, the new pastor apologized. The trustee admitted that he had been mad at first, but added, "Now I'm not mad. I wouldn't have wanted my dog to hear that sermon at any price."

• • •

SEXTONS

The sexton of a large church with meetings of one kind or another scheduled every day in various parts of the church had many extra demands shoved on him. Asked how he could maintain an even disposition with all the aggravations and complaints, he explained, "I just put my feelings in neutral and let them push me around."

• • •

After he was on the job for a few weeks, people discovered that the new sexton could play the piano very well. Every now and again he played for one of the weeknight services. Asked how he could do both jobs, he replied, "I watch my pews and keys."

• • •

Chapter 17

THE LAST LAUGH

God's laugh is the laugh of victory. As the devil surveyed the cross that dark Friday afternoon, he thought he had won. Jesus' head fell lifeless on His chest. A spear pierced His side. Roman authorities declared Him dead, and they buried Him. A large stone sealed the grave. Hell had triumphed.

But wait! God had a joke to play on Satan. "It's Friday, but Sunday's coming!" Early that first morning of the week He who had permitted His body to become a corpse seized the keys of death. A new proclamation broke the air, "He is risen!" Jesus exclaimed, "I am the Living One; I was dead, and behold I am alive for ever and ever!" (Rev. 1:18). His was the most amazing, unimaginable comeback story of all time.

Michelangelo made these strong remarks to his fellow painters in 1564: "Why do you keep filling gallery after gallery with endless pictures of Christ on the cross, Christ dying, Christ hanging dead? Let us see beyond it to the Easter dawn with its beams streaming upon the risen Christ, Christ alive,

Christ triumphant. That is the tonic we need to keep us happily upon our way laughing and singing and recklessly unafraid, because the feel of victory is in the air and our hearts thrill to it."

God knows how it will all turn out in the end. The last book in the Bible colorfully portrays the Second Coming of Christ in glory to subdue Satan and his cohorts, to establish his endless kingdom. Though men mock God now, someday He will have the last laugh. This has been termed "comic eschatology." "He who laughs last laughs best."

For 70 years atheistic communism sought to stifle the celebration of Easter in Russia. But in 1991, on the first Easter after the collapse of communism, Easter services were televised from Moscow's Cathedral of the Epiphany from midnight till past 4 a.m. with political leaders seen attending, greeting each other, "Christ is risen!" *Izvestia*, the government daily, asked in amazement, "Who could have thought even recently that the capital of our Fatherland, the bulwark of atheism, would dress up for Easter?"[29]

Eugene O'Neill wrote a play picturing Lazarus, raised from the dead by Jesus, going about laughing, "Fear is no more. There is no death." The crowds capture the mood of Lazarus, chanting as they march, "Laugh! Laugh with Lazarus. Fear is no more." Tradition says Lazarus' home in Bethany was called "The House of Laughter."[30]

Why should heaven-bound people look gloomy or grim? Perhaps a five-year-old's version of John 3:16 wasn't too far wrong when she ended it, "whoever believes in Him shall have everLAUGHING life."

• • •

GOLF

A church elder stepped to the first tee, took a mighty swing, and made a hole in one.

"How wonderful," said his pastor and playing partner. "Now I'll take my practice swing, and then we can start to play."

• • •

Billy Graham: "God answers my prayers everywhere—except on the golf course."

• • •

A church stopped buying from its regular office supply dealer. They ordered pew pencils from a new dealer. The next Sunday when visitors were asked to register, they picked up pencils stamped with the words, "PLAY GOLF NEXT SUNDAY."

• • •

MONEY

During a sharing period in the early part of a service, a visitor admitted a shortcoming. "I'm a spendthrift. I just cannot keep any money in my pocket. I give it right away as if it grew on trees. Please pray for me."

"We certainly will," said the pastor, "right after the offering."

• • •

IRS (phoning a pastor): "Do you have a member by the name of Archibald Normanski?"

Pastor: "Yes, we do."

IRS: "Did he make a gift of two thousand dollars to your church last year?"

Pastor: "No, but call me tomorrow and he will have."

• • •

A family on vacation attended a church service with an unfamiliar order of worship. Two offerings were scheduled.

As the offering plate was passed for the second time, a young son asked his father, "Is this for the sales tax?"

• • •

As the congregation departed from the morning service, a beggar standing on the corner with outstretched hand could be heard repeating, "Folks, it's just a onetime gift. No follow-up phone calls. No monthly pledges to meet."

• • •

An unemployed preacher with a good build wanted to join the police force. The commissioner interviewed him, expressed satisfaction at his physical condition, then asked one final question, "What would you do to break up a rioting mob?"

The preacher thought a minute, then answered, "I'd announce an offering."

• • •

PREACHERS' WIVES

The Right Reverend Charles Francis Hall, Episcopal Bishop of New Hampshire, while attending the 1968 Lambeth Conference in London, was to attend a special service at Westminster Abbey. His wife, out shopping with another bishop's wife, realizing it was almost time for the service at the Abbey, jumped into a taxi and shouted at the driver, "Take us to the cathedral!"

He deposited them at the Roman Catholic cathedral. Not realizing where they were, the wives marched up to the usher, "We're bishops' wives. Where do we sit?"

No one recalls the response of the usher, but the whole

story made the front page of London newspapers the next day.

• • •

Commuters were hurrying to catch their early morning trains. A pastor's wife, who was also a school teacher, walking by the suburban station on her way to her class, noticed a lady slumped over the steering wheel of a car parked in the station lot, seemingly in distress. Feeling it her duty to offer help, the pastor's wife asked, "Anything wrong?"

The lady, half crying, half laughing, explained, "For 14 years I have driven my husband to the station to catch his 7 a.m. train. Today I forgot him."

• • •

A pastor attended a session on time management. Returning to his study, he decided to put the principles into practice.

Early next morning he wrote out his priorities for the day. Then he phoned his wife.

Then he rescheduled his priorities for the day.

• • •

Well-known Bible teacher Dr. Harry Ironside, driving home with his wife after a long and busy Sunday, said, "Please don't speak sharply to me. You must realize I have preached six sermons today."

She replied, "And you must realize I have listened to all six of them."

• • •

SUNDAY SCHOOL

A little boy forgot his lines in the Sunday school program. His mother tried to prompt him from the front seat by gestures and lip movement but to no avail. Finally, she leaned forward and whispered his cue, "I am the light of the world."

Smiling from ear to ear and in clear voice he boomed out, "My mother is the light of the world."

• • •

"Who put the stars in the sky?" asked the Sunday school teacher, reviewing the previous week's lesson.

"I know," said Johnny. "It was America."

"Why do you say it was America?" asked the surprised teacher.

"A lady sang about it in church," Johnny explained. "You know how the song goes, 'It took America to put the stars in place!'"

• • •

Newspaper item: The Senior Department of the First Presbyterian Sunday school will present *Hamlet* next Friday evening. No admission will be charged to see this tragedy in the church auditorium.

• • •

A teacher asked his Sunday school class, "Why did the priest and Levite pass by on the other side of the man who had been robbed?"

Little Butch, after serious thought, replied, "Because the poor man had already been robbed."

• • •

A little boy fell in love with his primary Sunday school teacher. On his way to Sunday school on her birthday, he picked a bouquet of straggly, bedraggled dandelions and daisies. Walking to her desk in front of the class, he handed her a note that read, "These flowers will fade, but you will smell forever."

• • •

The last laugh

Give us a sense of humor, Lord,
Give us the grace to laugh and smile;
But check our lips from needless jest
That what we speak
May be worthwhile.

—Anonymous

REFERENCE NOTES

1 Charles Haddon Spurgeon, *Lectures to My Students*, second series (London: Marshall Brothers, 1906), p. 118.

2 *The Joyful Noiseletter*, October 1992.

3 Dr. James Dobson, *Focus on the Family Bulletin*, May 1990.

4 Fuller Theological Seminary, 1958.

5 William R. Inge in Marchant's *Wit and Wisdom of Dean Inge*.

6 Norman Cousins, "The Laughter Prescription," *The Saturday Evening Post*, September 1990, p. 34.

7 Arthur T. Pierson, *Knowing the Scriptures*, reprint edition (Grand Rapids: Zondervan Publishing House, 1910), pp. 436-438.

8 Fulton J. Sheen, *Life Is Worth Living* (London: Peter Davies, 1954).

9 David C. McCasland, "My Search for Oswald Chambers," *Christianity Today*, October 4, 1993, p. 38.

10 Charles Swindoll, *Laugh Again* (Word Publishing, 1992), p. 193.

11 Norman Cousins, *Anatomy of an Illness* (New York: W. W. Norton Co., 1979).

12 Elisabeth Elliot, *Shadow of the Almighty: The Life and Testament of Jim Elliot* (New York: Harper, 1958), p. 78.

13 Paul Jewett, "Wit and Wisdom," *Christianity Today*, June 8, 1959, p. 9.

14 Beatrice C. Engstrand, *The Gift of Healing: A Legacy of Hope* (Wynwood Press, 1990), pp. 220-21.

15   G. K. Chesterton, *The Napoleon of Noting Hill* (New York: Paulist Press, 1978).

16   Donnie Radcliffe, *Simply Barbara Bush* (Warner Books, 1989).

17   George Casalis, *Portraits of Karl Barth*. Trans. by Robert McAfee Brown (Doubleday, 1963), p. 3.

18   William Zinsser, *On Writing Well*, third edition (Harper & Row,1986), pp.183-4.

19   Bill Hybels, Stuart Briscoe, and Haddon Robinson, *Mastering Contemporary Preaching* (Sisters: Multno-mah Publishers, 1990), p. 82.

20   Ralph Earle, *Word Meanings in the New Testament* (Peabody, MA: Hendrickson Publishers, 1997), p. 362.

21   Charles Stanford, *The Wit and Humor of Life* (London: Elliot Stock Publishing Co., 1886), p. 64.

22   Arthur B. Fowler, private correspondence, 1959.

23   Arthur T. Pierson, ibid., pp. 436-38.

24   Paul Jewett, chapel talk at Fuller Theological Seminary, 1958.

25   Associated Press, 2/15/2005.

26   Leonard Sweet, *The Prescription for a Healthy Life* (Nashville: Abingdon Press, 1996), pp. 20-2.

27   Henri Cormier, *The Humor of Jesus* (New York: Alba House, 1977), p. v.

28   G. Campbell Morgan, *The Gospel According to Luke* (New York: Revell, 1931), p. 277.

29   *The Joyful Noiseletter*, June-July 1994.

30   Eugene O'Neill, *Lazarus Laughed* (New York: Random House, Inc., 1941).